# Flavours of Rome

*Flavours of Italy*

CARLA BARDI

# ROME
## AND THE PROVINCES
## OF LAZIO

NH
NEW
HOLLAND

First published in 2000 by
New Holland Publishers (UK) Ltd
London • Cape Town • Sydney • Auckland

24 Nutford Place
London W1H 5DQ
United Kingdom

Level 1, Unit 4, 14 Aquatic Drive
Frenchs Forest, NSW 2086
Australia

80 McKenzie Street
Cape Town 8001
South Africa

Unit 1A, 218 Lake Road
Northcote, Auckland
New Zealand

ISBN 1 85974 558 X

This book was conceived, edited, and designed by
McRae Books Srl, Florence, Italy.

Text: Carla Bardi
Photography: Marco Lanza
Set Design: Rosalba Gioffrè
Design: Marco Nardi
Translation from the Italian: Linda Clearwater
Editing: Alison Leach, Anne McRae

2 4 6 8 10 9 7 5 3 1

Colour separations: Fotolito Toscana, Florence, Italy
Printed and bound by Mladinska Knjiga, Slovenia

# Contents

# Introduction

L azio lies in the heart of Italy, midway between Tuscany in the north and Campania in the south. Despite its position, its inhabitants have rather more in common with the fun-loving peoples of the south than the rather terse, businesslike Tuscans to the north. The abundant Roman table reflects its peoples' temperament, and the business of eating in the Eternal City has been pursued with zeal and a delight in the spectacular since the times of the Roman Empire.

We have all heard of Roman banquets where course upon course of flamboyantly absurd dishes were served, from fattened dormice, to sweet and sour peaches, and the tongues of flamingoes and nightingales, all bathed in rancid fish sauces heavily flavored with spices. Many of these far-fetched dishes probably come from Petronius's comic novel *Satyricon*, the most famous episode of which mocks the immensely rich but vulgar Trimalchio and the banquet he gave to impress friends and hangers-on in Nero's decadent Rome. The reality of day-to-day eating habits in ancient Rome was far more sober: breakfast was a hearty meal consisting at least in part of leftovers from the previous evening (cheese, bread, honey, eggs, and olives). Lunch was typically a light snack, taken in a city tavern or bought from any of the many street vendors. The main meal of the day was eaten at home in the evening, after a visit to the baths. A Roman dinner could start with a hearty soup made from cereals or legumes, or a platter of fresh vegetables. This might be followed by cheese, bread, milk, capers, and olives, with dried or fresh fruit to finish. Wealthier Romans might also have fish and, occasionally, meat. As Rome rose to its height and a few people became very rich, sumptuous evening banquets did become a part of the social and business scene. (For more information on food in ancient Rome see pages 66–67.)

*The earliest Roman cookbook, called* De Arte Coquinaria, *was left to us by Marcus Gavius Apicius who lived in the 1st century* AD. *Anecdotes abound about this extravagant fellow, who reputedly squandered a fortune and then poisoned himself rather than live in poverty.*

*Left: lamb, cheese, bread, vegetables, and wine – staples of a Roman kitchen.*
*Below: the Colosseum, symbol of Rome.*

*One of Italy's best known wine stories comes from Montefiascone, on the shores of Lake Bolsena in northern Lazio. There are many versions, but according to most it was a prelate from Augsburg in Germany who, before setting out on a journey to Rome, sent a servant ahead of him to locate the inns with the best wines on the way. This would determine his itinerary. His servant was instructed to mark inns with good wine on a map with the word Est! Those serving excellent wine could merit Est! Est!! When the faithful servant reached the village of Montefiascone, he found the local wine so good that he marked it as Est! Est!! Est!!! And so it remains to the present day.*

During the 5th century the Roman Empire finally collapsed under mounting pressure from invading Germanic and Slav peoples from the north and east. Rome itself was sacked several times and the last emperor, Augustulus was deposed in 476. The long medieval period was marked by food shortages and famine, and it was the poorer classes who suffered most.

An amusing insight into dining in this period has been left to us in a little book of table manners called the *Piccolo Galateo Conviviale del Medioevo*. Directed at the upper classes, its suggestions for good table manners include: not asking what's on the menu, not eating things from other peoples' plates, not spitting food out, not drinking too much, and remembering to say grace before the meal begins. Table manners must certainly have deteriorated after this, because another *galateo,* published in the 16th century, instructed would-be refined diners "not to scratch themselves at the table; to avoid spitting except when strictly necessary, in which case to do it elegantly (!); not to stuff too much food into one's mouth at a time since this could lead to hiccoughs or other unseemly noises; not to clean one's teeth with the tablecloth; not to rinse one's mouth out with wine and then spit it out; and not to place one's toothpick behind one's ear, as a barber might."

The power vacuum left by the end of imperial rule was gradually filled by the papacy. By the 14th century, when the papacy was reunited in Rome (after a period of double papacy, split between Avignon in Provence and Rome), the papal court won renown for the brillance of its banquets, at which elaborate foods and excellent wines were served. The growth in power of the papacy in Renaissance times was reflected in ever more splendid courtly banquets and, in particular, a real and detailed appreciation of the local wines.

However, it was only from the 16th century onward, with the arrival of products from the Americas, that the basis of Rome's present-day cooking tradition developed. The gradual introduction of tomatoes, potatoes, peppers,

*Dining in style with a view over the Eternal City.*

*Prosciutto and salami.*

eggplants (aubergines), corn, chocolate, sunflowers, turkey, and many other items changed the way people ate. Recipe books were written to help cooks to assimilate the new foods: the first book to explain corn and its uses, written by Virgilio Polidoro, was published in Rome in 1576.

Writers, artists, and travelers of every nation flocked to Rome on their Grand Tours in the 18th and 19th centuries. Many have left us detailed records of every aspect of the city's food and wine. Veteran English traveler Mariana Starke even made a minute list of the price of foodstuffs! Gogol, Berlioz, Stendhal, Goethe, Thorvaldson, and a multitude of others passed through the city: by their notes we learn that pasta was already an important component of any menu, that *Fritto Misto* (see recipe, page 76) was frequently served, and that the local cheeses – ricotta, percorino and mozzarella – were equally delicious then as they are today. The local wines were obviously imbibed by all, since everyone appears to have something to say about them, for better or for worse. In general, the travelers approved of the Roman table, reserving special praise for the local fruit and vegetables.

ITALY

*Lazio*

Viterbo

Rieti

ROME

TYRRHENIAN SEA

Frosinone

Latina

**Rome today**: although Lazio is a fairly large and populous region, three of its five million inhabitants live in the city of Rome. The others are scattered among 370 communes in the other four provinces. Rome, the capital of Italy, contains within its historical center the tiny but powerful state of the Vatican City, headquarters of the Roman Catholic Church. Rome is a cosmopolitan city, bustling with bureaucrats, government officials, and religious officials and pilgrims from every part of Italy and the world. Like all large cities, Roman restaurants offer a wide variety of excellent foods from every region of Italy and from other countries. Nonetheless, traditional Roman fare is still to be found, particularly away from the tourist spots. Remember too, that, unlike Florence or Venice whose local characters have in many ways been overwhelmed by mass tourism, Rome has a large enough local population to have kept its unique, fun-loving character and cuisine. A small deviation down any sidestreet or a trip outside the city center will bring you to a trattoria or *osteria* filled with locals enjoying the things they do best: eating and talking.

A traditional Roman meal will begin with *Bruschetta* (see recipe, page 15), *Fave con Pecorino* (see recipe, page 19), or *Carciofini Sott'Olio* (see recipe, page 18). This will be followed by a hearty and abundant first course, usually based on pasta. *Bucatini all'Amatriciana* (see recipe, page 29) and *Spaghetti alla Carbonara* (see recipe, page 32) are two you will find on every menu. Lamb is the most typical meat dish, prepared by roasting (*Abbacchio al Forno*; see recipe, page 65) or braising (*Abbacchio alla Romana*; see recipe, page 72). Side dishes will invariably include artichokes (*Carciofi alla Giudia*; see recipe, page 86) and peas (*Piselli alla Romana*; see recipe, page 85). If you can face it, the waiters will then offer you a choice from at least six homemade desserts from all over Italy. You will finish with an espresso and strong need for a siesta!

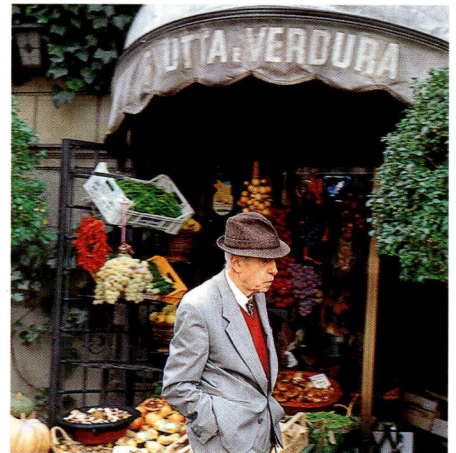

*Romans don't do all their shopping in supermarkets and the city abounds in tiny cheese, cured meat, and vegetable shops, their wares often sprawling out the door onto the street.*

*Rome's climate is highly conducive to outdoor dining, and cafés and trattorias flourish in the city from April until November. Dining on a sidewalk or tiny piazza on a hot summer night in Rome is one of life's great pleasures.*

*Fiumicino is an 18th-century fishing village on the outskirts of Rome. Fresh seafood is sold at the fish market along the port. Near the international airport, it is also a good, if crowded, place to take a swim in summer.*

*The castle of Tecchiena near the town of Alatri in Frosinone. The town itself, with its 4th-century BC walls and acropolis, is well worth a visit. A drive through the surrounding countryside, stopping off at a local trattoria for lunch, is a delightful way to spend a summer's day.*

Rome now sprawls across an area much larger even than it did in imperial times when the Romans ruled half the known world, from Palestine to England. It has encompassed the coastal towns of Ostia (the port of ancient Rome) and Fiumicino. Both make pleasant day trips away from the bustle and heat of the central city. On the other side of town lies Tivoli, which hosts the still-imposing ruins of the Emperor Hadrian's Villa and the wonderfully refreshing 16th-century Villa d'Este. The gardens are full of fountains and water spraying, running, and dribbling in all directions, while the sumptuous villa itself gives us some idea of the splendor the popes allowed themselves.

Although the outlying provinces are relatively small compared to Rome, they all offer their own special produce, dishes, and wines. Beginning in the southeast: **Frosinone** is the capital of the area known as the Ciociaria. Inhabited by the ancient Volsci people from around 600 BC, the town was conquered by Rome as it expanded during the 4th century BC. Nowadays the province is devoted to agriculture and light industry. Excellent prosciutto, salami, pecorino, lamb, peas, strawberries, olives, and olive oil are typical local produce. Our recipe for *Frittata alla Ciociara* (see recipe, page 80) comes from this area. Wine has been made here for at least 20 centuries; the first recorded description was made by Pliny the Elder. Originally sweet and bubbly, today's Cesenese wines are mainly dry. The monks at the beautiful Cistercian monastery of Trisulti at Collepardo produce some delicious herbal liqueurs.

**Latina** is the capital of this southern province, most of which was covered in inhospitable marshland from the Middle Ages until the 1940s, when it was successfully drained. The reclaimed land of the Pontine plains is now dedicated to market gardening, farming, and industry. Tomatoes, artichokes and other vegetables, cheese, and lamb are produced here. The many ancient towns along the coast serve some excellent seafood. The wonderful sweet and sour dish *Tiella con Pesce* (see recipe, page 47) comes from Gaeta in the south. The cooking in this area has much in common with the nearby city of Naples. The local wines, from Cori, Aprilia, and the south, were not widely known outside the area until recently. In the last ten years or so, some have been exported, even as far afield as North America. Most are simple dry or medium whites and reds, which team up beautifully with the local foods.

The northern province of **Viterbo** is home to many ancient Etruscan towns: Tuscania, Viterbo, Tarquinia, and Cerveteri were all important centers of Etruscan culture. This is also the province of Lake Bolsena, the largest lake in Italy. Local dishes include many based on eels and trout from the lake. Some of Lazio's best wines are produced along the shores of the lake. The area is also known for its cherries, strawberries, pears, figs, and other fruits. Farther south, the area around Lake Bracciano produces some of the region's best cured meats. Fish and seafood are popular along the coast. The coastal town of Civitavecchia is also the hometown of a rather complicated but delicious traditional cake – *Pizza Dolce Civitavecchiese* (see recipe, page 106) Gastronomically Viterbo is a varied province, sharing many dishes and traditions with Rome, but also with Tuscany and Umbria.

The inland province of **Rieti** came to Lazio from Umbria and its gastronomy reflects its historical ties. It also has strong ties with neighboring Abruzzo. However, we shouldn't forget that this is the zone which gave Rome one of its most famous dishes – *Bucatini all'Amatriciana* (see recipe, page 29). The dish is named for the town of Amatrice in the extreme northeast of the province. This area also produces good lamb, kid, ricotta, pecorino, and cured meats. Black truffles are also found here in the fall.

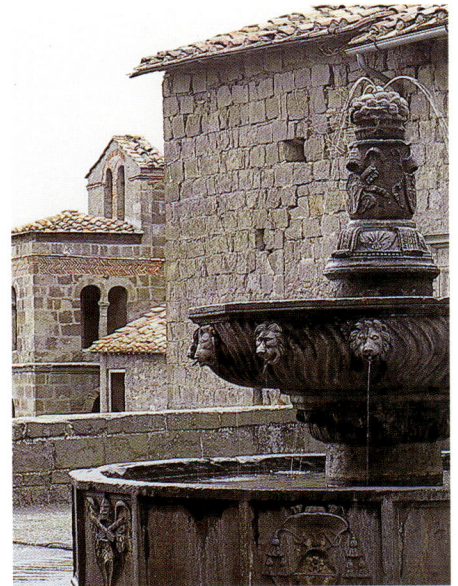

*Fountain in the courtyard of the 13th-century Papal Palace at Viterbo. The city has a beautiful medieval center which, although badly damaged during World War II, has been carefully restored.*

*The deserted coastlines of Latina are great places to get away from it all, either on foot or horseback.*

# Antipasti

Roman cooking is essentially simple and rustic and the few typical appetizers reflect this tradition. A special meal could begin with a platter of locally cured meats (salami, prosciutto, and ham), olives, pickled vegetables, preserved artichokes, and a selection of crostini (toasted breads with different toppings). Toasted Bread with Garlic and Oil is the most classic crostino. These dishes are all rooted in the region's peasant origins – the above list could be a typical plowman's lunch of a century ago. Other more elaborate classics include pancakes with pecorino or meat sauce, Fried Mozzarella Sandwiches, and Stuffed Fried Zucchini Flowers.

# Bruschetta

## *Toasted Bread with Garlic and Oil*

Toast the bread until golden brown on both sides. ❧ Rub half a garlic clove evenly over each slice. The crisp toast works like a grater. Drizzle with the oil and season with salt and pepper to taste. Serve hot.

*Serves 4*
*Preparation: 5 minutes*
*Cooking: 5 minutes*
*Recipe grading: easy*

- 4–8 slices day-old, firm-textured bread
- 2–4 cloves garlic, peeled
- 4–8 tablespoons high-quality extra-virgin olive oil
- salt to taste
- freshly ground black pepper

*Suggested wine: a dry white*
*(Frascati Secco)*

*Bruschetta is a common appetizer throughout central Italy, but the Romans claim to have invented it. For a successful dish you must use only the freshest and best quality extra-virgin olive oil. Choose a dark green, translucent oil from a good specialty store. Be sure to check the expiry date on the bottle; even the best olive oil keeps only for about a year. Never buy oil that doesn't carry a production or expiry date.*

*Serves 4*
*Preparation: 20 minutes*
*Cooking: about 1 hour*
*Recipe grading: fairly easy*

- ¼ cup/1 oz/30 g dried porcini mushrooms
- 2 cups/16 fl oz/500 ml cold water
- 5 large, very ripe tomatoes, peeled
- 1 stick/4 oz/125 g butter, chopped
- salt to taste
- 2 cups/12 oz/350 g rice (Italian semifino or fino)
- ½ cup/2 oz/60 g freshly grated parmesan cheese
- 2 eggs
- 1 small onion, finely chopped
- 1 stalk celery, finely chopped
- 1¼ cups/5 oz/150 g ground beef
- 4 chicken livers, finely chopped
- ½ cup/2 oz/60 g prosciutto, finely chopped
- 3½ oz/100 g mozzarella cheese, diced in ½-inch/1-cm cubes
- scant 2 cups/3½ oz/100 g fresh breadcrumbs
- 1–2 cups/8–16 fl oz/250–500 ml olive oil for frying

*Suggested wine: a dry white*
*(Frascati Superiore)*

# Supplì alla Romana

## *Filled Rice Balls*

Place the mushrooms in a small bowl and cover with warm water. Leave to soften for about 20 minutes. ❧ Put the cold water, 4 chopped tomatoes, three-quarters of the butter, and salt in a large saucepan. Bring to a boil and add the rice. Stir frequently and cook until the rice is ready. ❧ Remove from the heat and stir in the parmesan and the eggs. Spread the mixture out on a large plate to cool. ❧ In the meantime, drain the mushrooms and chop coarsely. Heat the remaining butter in a small skillet (frying pan) and sauté the mushrooms with the onion, celery, beef, chicken livers, and prosciutto for 4–5 minutes over a medium heat. ❧ Add the remaining chopped tomato and season with salt to taste. Cover and cook over a low heat for about 20 minutes, or until the sauce has reduced. Stir frequently so that the sauce doesn't stick. ❧ Use a tablespoon to scoop up some rice and shape it into a ball about the size of an egg. Make a hollow in the ball of rice and fill with the meat sauce and one or two cubes of cheese. Seal with a little more rice. Roll the filled rice ball in the breadcrumbs and set it aside on a plate. Repeat until all the rice, meat sauce, and cheese have been used. ❧ Heat the oil in a large skillet pan until very hot, but not smoking. Fry the rice balls until crisp and golden brown all over. ❧ Drain on paper towels and serve immediately.

*For a lighter dish, fry the rice balls in batches of 5–6. The temperature of the oil should not drop too much when you add the rice balls. This stops them from absorbing too much oil. Supplì make a very hearty appetizer; you may prefer to serve it as a first course or even as a main course with a salad.*

*Serves 4*

*Preparation: 20 minutes + 2 months'
  preserving*

*Cooking: 10 minutes*

*Recipe grading: easy*

- 8–12 fresh globe artichokes
- juice of 1 lemon
- 8½ cups/3½ pints/2 liters cold water
- 8 tablespoons white wine vinegar
- salt to taste
- extra-virgin olive oil

*Suggested wine: a light, dry white
  (Colli Albani Secco)*

*Delicious served on their own, these
tasty little hearts are also good with
a platter or sliced, cured meats
(salami, ham, prosciutto).*

# Carciofini Sott'Olio

## *Artichokes Preserved in Oil*

Clean the artichokes by trimming the tops and stalks. Remove all the tough outer leaves so that only the pale, tender hearts remain. Place in a bowl of cold water with the lemon juice for 15 minutes. ❧ Bring the water, vinegar, and salt to a boil in a large saucepan. Drain the artichokes and add to the saucepan. Cook for 10 minutes. ❧ Drain the artichokes and dry well with paper towels. Transfer to clean preserving jars and cover with oil. Seal the jars and set aside in a cool, dark place for at least 2 months before serving.

# Fave con Pecorino

## *Fava Beans with Ewe's Cheese*

Rinse the beans thoroughly under cold running water. Dry well on a clean dishcloth. Discard any tough or whithered looking pods, or any with ugly spots or marks. Place in an attractive serving dish. ❧ Serve with the cheese already cut into dice, or in a wedge cut from the round.

*Serves 6–8*
*Preparation: 5 minutes*
*Recipe grading: easy*

- 4 lb/2 kg fresh, young fava beans/broad beans in their pods
- 8½–12 oz/250–350 g pecorino romana ewe's cheese

*Suggested wine: a dry, aromatic white (Bianco Capena)*

*Fava beans arrive in the markets in Italy in the early spring. For several weeks, while the beans are at their freshest, they are a daily offering on the tables of many trattorias and private homes. They are equally good served at the end of the meal.*

Serves: 4

Preparation: 10 minutes + 1 hour's
   resting

Cooking: 15 minutes

Recipe grading: fairly easy

- 4 large, thin slices of firm-textured bread
- freshly ground black pepper
- 12 oz/350 g mozzarella cheese, sliced
- 4 anchovy fillets, crumbled (optional)
- scant 1 cup/7 fl oz/200 ml milk
- 1 cup/4 oz/125 g all-purpose/plain flour
- 2 eggs
- dash of salt
- 1–2 cups/8–16 fl oz/250–500 ml olive oil for frying

Suggested wine: a dry white
   (Orvieto)

# Pandorato Ripieno
## *Fried Mozzarella Sandwiches*

Remove the crusts from the bread and cut each slice in halves or quarters. Sprinkle with pepper. ❧ Cover half the bread with the mozzarella slices and the anchovies, if using. Place the remaining slices of bread over the top to make little sandwiches. ❧ Dip the sandwiches briefly into the milk, then sprinkle well with flour. Arrange the sandwiches on a large plate. ❧ Beat the eggs with the salt and pour over the sandwiches. Leave for about 1 hour so that the egg is completely absorbed. ❧ Heat the oil in a large skillet (frying pan) until very hot, but not smoking. Fry the sandwiches a few at a time until they are deep golden brown all over. Drain well and place on paper towels. ❧ Serve hot.

*This hearty appetizer also makes a nourishing snack or light lunch.*

# The Wines of Lazio

Lazio can probably boast the longest unbroken winemaking tradition in the world. The Etruscans, who inhabited the area 800 years BC, were already experienced vinters. The Romans inherited their traditions and huge quantities of locally grown wine were consumed in the halycon days of the empire. Served with water, it was the most common drink and appeared on the table at all mealtimes. During the Renaissance, the popes maintained a lively interest in wine, both local and imported. Today Lazio is known for its white wines, most of which are produced in the Alban Hills and Aprilia near Rome. To the north, around the beautiful Lake Bolsena, some excellent whites are also produced. To the west, on the coast at Cerveteri, some of the region's best reds are made.

*The Alban hills encircle the city of Rome on three sides. It is here, in the six DOC zones, that most of Lazio's white wines are made. The northern hills are known as the Castelli Romani, and the central and southern parts as the Colli Albani. Frascati, Colli Albani, Velletri and Zagarolo are the best-known wines from here. To the north, Est! Est!! Est!!! di Montefiascone, was named by a papal envoy sent to test the local wines and told to code the best as Est! This one was so good that it merited three!*

The best reds in Lazio are produced in the coastal region of Cerveteri. The Ciociaria area, east of the Alban Hills, is also best known for its reds.

Lazio makes its share of spumante and sweet dessert wines. Aleatico di Gradoli, similar to port, is the oldest of these. The area has responded to the increasing demand for bubblies by producing dozens of them.

In days of old, the wines from the Alban Hills were brought into Rome by horse and cart. Stories abound of the mischief and fun the journey involved, and Roman cuisine even has recipes dedicated to these loyal workers.

The Castelli Romani zone takes its name from the beautiful castles that dot the hillsides. Many are owned by winegrowers and operate as cellars. This is the Aldobrandini castle at Lucina.

*Serves 4–6*
*Preparation: 5 minutes*
*Cooking: 25 minutes*
*Recipe grading: easy*

- 3 eggs
- salt to taste
- 1¼ cups/5 oz/150 g all-purpose/plain white flour
- scant ½ cup/3½ fl oz/100 ml milk, warm
- 3–4 tablespoons butter or extra-virgin olive oil
- 1 cup/4 oz/125 g freshly grated pecorino romano cheese

*Suggested wine: a dry white*
*(Orvieto)*

# Pizzacce

## *Pancakes with Ewe's Cheese*

Beat the eggs with the salt. ❧ Stir in the flour, then add the milk and stir to obtain a smooth batter. It should be about the consistency of pancake batter. If necessary, add more milk or flour to obtain the right consistency. ❧ Heat the butter or oil in a small skillet (frying pan) until very hot. Add 1–2 tablespoons of batter and twirl the pan so that it spreads evenly across the bottom. Cook until brown, then toss to brown the other side. Repeat until all the batter is used up. ❧ Sprinkle the fritters with pecorino and serve hot.

*This Roman version of savory pancakes is a favorite with children and adults alike.*

# Pizzacce di Rieti

*Baked Pancakes with Meat Sauce*

Prepare the meat sauce. ❧ Prepare the Pizzacce. ❧ Roll the pancakes loosely and arrange them in an ovenproof baking dish. Spoon the sauce over the top and sprinkle with the pecorino. Season with cayenne or chile pepper, if liked. ❧ Bake in a preheated oven at 400°F/200°C/gas 6 for 10 minutes, or until the cheese is light, golden brown. ❧ Serve hot.

*Serves: 4–6*

*Preparation: 5 minutes + time to make the meat sauce and pancakes*

*Cooking: about 10 minutes*

*Recipe grading: easy*

- 1 quantity Meat sauce (choose from: sausage sauce on page 34, the mushroom and liver sauce on page 38, or the clove-flavored meat sauce on page 48)
- 1 quantity Pizzacce – see recipe, facing page
- 1¼ cups/5 oz/150 g freshly grated pecorino romano cheese
- dash of cayenne or chile pepper (optional)

*Suggested wine: a dry red (Velletri Rosso Secco)*

*These pancakes make a warming winter appetizer. They are quite filling so you won't need to serve a first course afterward.*

# Fiori di Zucca Farciti

## *Stuffed Fried Zucchini Flowers*

Rinse the flowers carefully under cold running water. Trim the stalks and dry the flowers carefully with paper towels. ✎ Mix the anchovies with the breadcrumbs in a bowl. Add the parsley, 1 egg, and salt and pepper to taste (since the anchovies are already salty, you may not need much salt). Mix well. ✎ Use this mixture to carefully stuff the flowers. ✎ Beat the remaining eggs and place them in a shallow bowl. Place the flour in a shallow bowl and dip the stuffed flowers first in the flour, then in the egg. ✎ Heat the oil in a large skillet (frying pan) until very hot, but not smoking. Fry the flowers in batches of 5–6 at a time. Turn them so that they brown all over. Drain on paper towels. Repeat until all the flowers are cooked. Sprinkle with a little salt, if liked. ✎ Serve hot.

*Serves 4*
*Preparation: 10 minutes*
*Cooking: 15 minutes*
*Recipe grading: fairly easy*

- 20 fresh zucchini/courgette flowers
- 6 anchovy fillets, crumbled
- 2 cups/4 oz/125 g fine breadcrumbs
- 1 tablespoon finely chopped parsley
- 3 eggs
- salt to taste
- freshly ground black pepper
- $^3/_4$ cup/3 oz/90 g all-purpose/plain flour
- 1–2 cups/8–16 fl oz/250–500 ml olive oil for frying

*Suggested wine: a dry, fruity white (Colli Albani Secco)*

*The anchovies give this recipe a little extra zing. However, if you don't like them you may leave them out. The dish will be a little blander, but delicious all the same.*

# Primi piatti

Rome has a wide variety of pasta dishes and first courses of all kinds. This is the hometown of a thick type of spaghetti with a hollowed-out middle called "*bucatini*". They are served most often *all'Amatriciana* which is a spicy tomato sauce named for a town in the hills above the city (see next page). Other pasta favorites include *alla Carbonara* with an egg and bacon sauce, and the very simple garlic and oil, or pecorino cheese and pepper sauces. There are also many tasty soups made with vegetables or eggs, plus two types of gnocchi. Rice is not grown in Lazio and not widely used in the kitchen. However, I have included a scrumptious Papal Rice Mold for special occasions.

# Bucatini all'Amatriciana

## *Bucatini with Spicy Tomato and Pancetta Sauce*

Place a large pot of cold water over a high heat. ∾ Sauté the pancetta in the oil for 2–3 minutes. Add the chili pepper and onion, if using, and sauté for 2–3 minutes more. ∾ Pour in the wine and cook for 2–3 minutes until the wine evaporates. Season with salt and pepper. ∾ Peel the tomatoes and dice them. Add to the sauté pan and cook over a medium heat for about 15 minutes, or until the tomatoes have reduced. ∾ When the water in the pot is boiling, add the coarse sea salt, then the bucatini and cook for the time indicated on the package. ∾ Drain the pasta when it is cooked *al dente* and transfer to a large heated serving dish. Pour the sauce over the top and sprinkle with the cheese. Toss well and serve.

*Serves 4*
*Preparation: 10 minutes*
*Cooking: 25 minutes*
*Recipe grading: easy*

- $3/4$ cup/5 oz/150 g pancetta, diced
- 2 tablespoons extra-virgin olive oil
- $1/2$ teaspoon crushed chili pepper
- 1 onion, optional
- $1/4$ cup/2 fl oz/60 ml dry white wine
- salt to taste
- freshly ground black pepper
- 1 lb/500 g ripe tomatoes
- 2 tablespoons coarse sea salt
- 1 lb/500 g bucatini pasta
- 4 tablespoons freshly grated pecorino cheese

*Suggested wine: a dry white (Frascati Secco)*

*This recipe takes its name from Amatrice, a lovely town in the hills of the province of Rieti.*

# Spaghetti alla Puttanesca
## *Hot and Spicy Spaghetti with Black Olives*

Place a large pot of cold water over a high heat. ❧ Peel the tomatoes and dice them. Stone and chop about three-quarters of the olives. ❧ Heat the oil in a skillet (frying pan) and sauté the garlic with the chili pepper. Discard the garlic when it has turned light gold. Add the anchovies (if using) and stir well in the oil until they dissolve. ❧ Add the olives and capers, then the tomatoes. Season with salt and pepper (the anchovies and olives are both quite salty, so be sure to taste the sauce before seasoning). Cook over a medium-low heat for about 15 minutes, or until the sauce reduces. ❧ When the water in the pot is boiling, add the coarse sea salt, then the spaghetti and cook for the time indicated on the package. ❧ Drain the pasta when it is cooked *al dente* and transfer to a large heated serving dish. Pour the sauce over the top, toss well, and serve.

*Serves 4*
*Preparation: 10 minutes*
*Cooking: 25 minutes*
*Recipe grading: easy*

- 1 lb/500 g ripe tomatoes
- 8 oz/250 g black olives
- 2 tablespoons extra-virgin olive oil
- 2 cloves garlic, peeled and whole
- $\frac{1}{2}$ teaspoon crushed chili pepper
- 4 anchovy fillets (optional)
- 2 tablespoons capers
- salt to taste
- freshly ground black pepper
- 2 tablespoons coarse sea salt
- 1 lb/500 g spaghetti

*Suggested wine: a dry white*
*(Castelli Romani)*

*This fiery dish is named after the not very polite Italian word "puttana", which refers to women practicing the oldest profession in the world. The anchovies are not optional in the classic recipe, although since many people don't like their taste, they can be left out.*

*Serves 4*

*Preparation: 10 minutes*

*Cooking: about 15 minutes*

*Recipe grading: easy*

- $^3/_4$ cup/5 oz/150 g smoked pancetta or bacon, diced
- 1 tablespoon extra-virgin olive oil
- 1 clove garlic, lightly crushed but still whole
- 2 tablespoons coarse sea salt
- 1 lb/500 g spaghetti
- 5 eggs
- $3^1/_2$ tablespoons light/single cream (optional)
- salt to taste
- 4 tablespoons each freshly grated parmesan and pecorino cheese
- freshly ground black pepper

*Suggested wine: a light, dry rosé (Castelli Romani Rosato)*

# Spaghetti alla Carbonara

*Spaghetti with Egg and Bacon Sauce*

Place a large pot of cold water over a high heat. ➷ Sauté the pancetta or bacon in the oil with the garlic. Discard the garlic when it has turned pale gold. ➷ When the water in the pot is boiling, add the coarse sea salt, then the spaghetti and cook for the time indicated on the package. ➷ While the spaghetti is cooking, beat the eggs with the cream (if using), a dash of salt, the cheeses, and a generous grinding of pepper in a large bowl. ➷ Drain the pasta very thoroughly when it is cooked *al dente* and transfer to the bowl with the egg mixture. Add the pancetta or bacon and the oil and toss vigorously over a low heat for 2 minutes. Serve at once.

*This dish is said to have been invented during the last days of World War II. When US troops arrived in Rome, they brought an abundant supply of eggs and bacon which ingenious local cooks used to make the now classic Roman Carbonara.*

# Spaghetti Aglio e Olio

## *Spaghetti with Garlic and Oil Sauce*

*Serves 4*
*Preparation: 5 minutes*
*Cooking: about 15 minutes*
*Recipe grading: easy*

- 3 cloves garlic, lightly crushed
- ½ cup/4 fl oz/125 ml extra-virgin olive oil
- 2 tablespoons coarse sea salt
- 1 lb/500 g spaghetti
- freshly ground black pepper (optional)

*Suggested wine: a dry, fruity white (Colli Albani Secco)*

Place a large pot of cold water over a high heat. ❧ Heat the oil in a skillet (frying pan) and sauté the garlic until pale gold. ❧ When the water in the pot is boiling, add the coarse sea salt, then the spaghetti and cook for the time indicated on the package. ❧ Drain the pasta when it is cooked *al dente* and transfer to the skillet with the garlic and oil. Season with a generous grinding of pepper, if liked. Toss over a low heat for 1 minute. Serve hot.

*Another classic dish has exactly the same ingredients as this one, with the addition of about ½ teaspoon of crushed chili peppers.*

# Polenta sulla Spianatoia
## *Polenta with Sausage Sauce*

Serves 6
*Preparation: 10 minutes*
*Cooking: 50 minutes*
*Recipe grading: fairly easy*

- 3 tablespoons lard (or butter)
- 1 onion, finely chopped
- 1 stalk celery, finely chopped
- 1 small carrot, finely chopped
- 2 tablespoons finely chopped flat-leaf parsley
- 1 tablespoon concentrated tomato paste dissolved in $^1/_2$ cup/4 fl oz/ 125 ml cold water
- salt to taste
- 10 oz/300 g Italian sausage
- scant 3 quarts/4$^3/_4$ pints/2.75 liters cold water
- 1 tablespoon coarse sea salt
- 4$^1/_2$ cups/1 lb/500 g finely ground cornmeal/polenta

*Suggested wine: a young, full-bodied red (Sangiovese di Aprilia)*

Melt the lard in a skillet (frying pan) and sauté the onion, celery, carrot, and parsley over a medium heat until the vegetables are soft. ❧ Add the tomato paste and water, season with salt, then cover the skillet and cook over a medium-low heat for about 30 minutes. ❧ Peel the sausage and chop coarsely. Add to the vegetables and cook for 15 minutes more. ❧ Meanwhile prepare the polenta: bring the water to a boil with the sea salt. Gradually sprinkle in the cornmeal while stirring continuously with a large balloon whisk to stop lumps from forming. ❧ Cook over a low heat, stirring continuously for about 40 minutes. ❧ When cooked, turn out onto a polenta board (or large serving platter) and spoon the sauce over the top. ❧ Serve hot.

*Polenta originally comes from northern Italy, but has now spread to every region. This recipe is popular in Lazio during the winter months.*

# Pecorino and Ricotta Cheese

Rome was founded by pastoralists during the 8th century BC, so cheese-making is one of the region's most ancient gastronomic traditions. Ancient Roman writers have left records of several cheeses, including those from Vestino, Trebula, and Luni, as well as a smoked variety from Velabrum (these are all areas of ancient Latium). Cheese was an important source of protein during Classical times when meat was too expensive for most people. Ancient Roman cheeses were mostly made from the milk of sheep and goats. Many were served warm, perhaps after being cooked in the oven or over a grill. Cheeses were also mixed with crushed wheat and water to make savory breads or flavored with herbs and garlic and spread over bread to make a sort of ancient focaccia. Lazio is still an

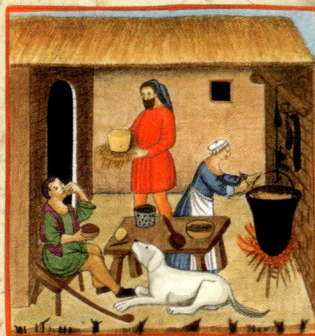

*This miniature shows ricotta cheese being made in late medieval times. During the latter half of the 20th century, cheesemaking changed from being a largely farm-based occupation to a flourishing local industry. Milk from many farms is now collected and sent to factories where larger quantites of consistently high-quality cheese is produced to European standards for consumption in Italy and abroad.*

important cheese-producing region. Pecorino romano, made from ewes' milk, is probably the best known of the local cheeses and is a major export item. Fresh creamy ricotta, also made from ewes' milk, is the other local favorite, although a variety of different cheeses are also produced. Caciotta, caciottone, and provatura are three of the better known traditional cheeses. They are not well known outside Lazio itself.

*Flocks of ewes thrive in among the olive groves that dot the landscape of Lazio. Their tasty milk is used to make both ricotta and pecorino cheese.*

*Forms of authentic pecorino romano bear a special brand (right) to show that they have been made within the designated area. This area now includes the provinces of Frosinone, Latina, Roma, and Viterbo, as well as parts of southern Tuscany and all of the island of Sardinia.*

The art of making ricotta cheese was re-introduced to Lazio after the fall of the Roman Empire by Saint Francis of Assisi. While this cheese is made throughout Italy, the Roman variety is slightly drier and more compact than the one produced in other regions.

Pecorino romano is a salty, aromatic cheese. Well-aged it makes an ideal grating cheese, while the younger varieties are served as table cheeses. The hefty forms – each one weighs about 50 lb (25 kg) – are produced from October through July each year and are aged for anywhere between four to twelve months.

Forms and containers of ricotta and pecorino cheese ready for eating or aging.

# Fettuccine alla Romana
## *Roman-Style Fettuccine*

*Serves 4*

*Preparation: 20 minutes (if using homemade fettuccine, + time to make it)*

*Cooking: 30 minutes*

*Recipe grading: easy*

- 1 lb/500 g fresh homemade or store-bought fettuccine (to make the pasta see recipe, page 49)
- salt to taste
- 4 tablespoons freshly grated pecorino cheese

For the sauce:
- 2 tablespoons dried porcini mushrooms
- 3 tablespoons coarsely chopped pork fat
- 1 small onion, finely chopped
- 1 clove garlic, finely chopped
- 14 oz/400 g fresh or canned peeled and chopped tomatoes
- salt and freshly ground black pepper to taste
- 8 oz/250 g trimmed, diced chicken livers
- ¹/₂ stick/2 oz/60 g butter
- 4 tablespoons dry white wine
- ¹/₂ cup/4 fl oz/125 ml broth (homemade or bouillon cube)

*Suggested wine: a dry red (Sangiovese)*

Prepare the fettuccine (if using homemade pasta). ❧ Place a large pot of cold, salted water over a high heat. ❧ Place the mushrooms in a small bowl of warm water and leave to soften for 15 minutes. ❧ Melt the pork fat in a skillet (frying pan) over a moderate heat and sauté the onion and garlic. ❧ Drain the mushrooms and add to the sauce together with the tomatoes. Season with salt and pepper. Cook for about 15 minutes over a moderate heat, or until the sauce reduces. ❧ Clean the chicken livers, cutting off and discarding any stringy membranes. Chop coarsely. ❧ Melt half the butter in a small, heavy-bottomed pan and cook the chicken livers over a moderate heat for 4–5 minutes. Pour in the wine and cook until it evaporates. ❧ Add the broth, then cover and cook over a low heat until the chicken livers are well-cooked (about 15 minutes). ❧ Add the chicken livers to the tomato sauce. ❧ When the water in the pot is boiling, add the fettuccine and cook for 3–5 minutes, if homemade (or the time indicated on the package, if store-bought). ❧ Drain the fettuccine and transfer to a heated serving bowl. Add the sauce and toss vigorously for 1–2 minutes. ❧ Sprinkle with the cheese and serve at once.

*If preparing the pasta at home, the fettuccine should be cut about ¹/₂ in/1 cm in width.*

# Spaghetti Cacio e Pepe
## *Spaghetti with Cheese and Pepper*

Serves 4
Preparation: 5 minutes
Cooking: about 10 minutes
Recipe grading: easy

- 2 tablespoons coarse sea salt
- 1 lb/500 g spaghetti
- 1¼ cups/5 oz/150 g freshly grated pecorino cheese
- freshly ground black pepper

*Suggested wine: a young, dry red (Frascati Novello)*

Place a large pot of cold water over a high heat. ❧ When the water is boiling, add the coarse sea salt, then the spaghetti and cook for the time indicated on the package. ❧ Drain the pasta when it is cooked *al dente,* leaving just a little more water than usual. This will help to melt the cheese and will prevent the pasta from sticking together. ❧ Transfer the spaghetti to a large heated serving dish. Sprinkle the pecorino over the top. Cover with a generous grinding of pepper and toss energetically for 1–2 minutes. ❧ Serve at once.

# Spaghetti al Tonno

*Spaghetti with Tuna Fish and Tomato Sauce*

Place a large pot of cold water over a high heat. ❧ Sauté the garlic and parsley in the oil in a large skillet (frying pan) over a moderate heat for 3–4 minutes. ❧ Add the tomatoes, season with salt and pepper, and cook for 15 minutes, or until the sauce reduces. ❧ When the water in the pot is boiling, add the coarse sea salt, then the spaghetti, and cook for the time indicated on the package. ❧ Mix the tuna into the tomato sauce, stir well, then remove from the heat. ❧ Drain the pasta when it is cooked *al dente* and transfer to a large heated serving dish. Add the tomato and tuna sauce and toss vigorously for 1–2 minutes. ❧ Serve at once.

*Serves 4*
*Preparation: 10 minutes*
*Cooking: about 15 minutes*
*Recipe grading: easy*

- 2 cloves garlic, finely chopped
- 2 tablespoons finely chopped flat-leaf parsley
- 4 tablespoons extra-virgin olive oil
- 6 large ripe tomatoes, peeled and diced
- salt to taste
- freshly ground black pepper
- 2 tablespoons coarse sea salt
- 1 lb/500 g spaghetti
- 8 oz/250 g tuna fish, packed in oil, drained, and flaked

*Suggested wine: a dry white*
*(Vignanello Bianco Secco)*

*This sauce is easy to prepare and very tasty. It goes well with spaghetti, but perhaps even better with the smaller spaghettini.*

# Tagliatelle con Prosciutto e Piselli

## *Tagliatelle with Prosciutto and Peas*

Prepare the tagliatelle (if using homemade pasta). ❧ Place a large pot of cold water over a high heat. ❧ Cook the peas in a small pot of lightly salted water until just cooked. Drain and set aside. ❧ Melt the butter in a skillet (frying pan) and sauté the onion and prosciutto for 5 minutes. ❧ Add the peas and season with salt and pepper. Leave to cook for 5 minutes. ❧ When the water is boiling, add the coarse sea salt, then the tagliatelle and cook for 5–7 minutes, or until cooked *al dente.* This depends on the type of tagliatelle used. Fresh tagliatelle takes a lot less time to cook than the dried store-bought type. ❧ Drain the tagliatelle and transfer to a heated serving dish. Sprinkle with the parmesan and serve at once.

*Serves 4*

*Preparation: 10 minutes (if using homemade tagliatelle, + time to make it)*

*Cooking: about 20 minutes*

*Recipe grading: easy*

- 1 lb/500 g fresh homemade or store-bought tagliatelle (to make the pasta see recipe, page 49)
- 2 cups/10 oz/300 g fresh (shelled weight) or frozen peas
- salt to taste
- $\frac{1}{2}$ stick/2 oz/60 g butter
- 1 small onion, finely chopped
- 4 oz/125 g prosciutto, cut in one thick slice and diced
- 6 tablespoons freshly grated parmesan cheese
- freshly ground black pepper
- 2 tablespoons coarse sea salt

*Suggested wine: a dry white (Est! Est!! Est!!!)*

*To make the pasta at home, follow the instructions on page 49. The tagliatelle should be cut about $\frac{1}{4}$ in/6 mm in width.*

# Timballo del Papa
*Papal Rice Mold*

*Serves 4*
*Preparation: 15 minutes*
*Cooking: about 40 minutes*
*Recipe grading: fairly easy*

- 10 oz/300 g chicken livers
- scant $^3/_4$ stick/2$^1/_2$ oz/75 g butter
- 1 medium onion, finely chopped
- 4 tablespoons dry white wine
- 2 cups/10 oz/300 g peeled and diced fresh or canned tomatoes
- salt to taste
- freshly ground black pepper
- 2$^1/_4$ cups/14 oz/400 g rice
- 4$^1/_4$ cups/1$^3/_4$ pints/1 liter meat broth (homemade or bouillon cube), boiling
- 4 tablespoons freshly grated parmesan cheese

*Suggested wine: a dry red (Cerveteri Rosso)*

Clean the chicken livers, cutting off and discarding any stringy membranes Chop coarsely. ❧ Heat two-thirds of the butter in a deep-sided skillet (frying pan) and sauté the onion until pale gold. ❧ Add the chicken livers and stir until they are brown. ❧ Pour in the wine and cook until it has evaporated Add the tomatoes and cook for 15 minutes, or until the sauce reduces. Season with salt and pepper. ❧ Add the rice and a little broth. Keep stirring and adding broth until the rice is cooked *al dente*. ❧ Remove the skillet from the heat and stir in the parmesan. ❧ Grease the sides of a ring mold with the remaining butter. Transfer the rice mixture to the mold and press down well. ❧ Bake in a preheated oven at 400°F/200°C/gas 6 for 10 minutes. ❧ Turn the baked mold out onto a heated platter and serve at once.

*With the exception of one or two seafood dishes, risottos are not typical of Lazio and the few recipes featuring rice are usually soups. This rather elaborate Pope's Rice Pie is reserved for very special occasions.*

# Tiella con Pesce
## *Sweet and Sour Squid Pie*

*Serves 4*
*Preparation: 30 minutes + 1 hour's rising*
*Cooking: about 1 hour*
*Recipe grading: fairly easy*

Crumble the yeast into a small bowl and add the sugar and half the water, stirring until the yeast dissolves. ❧ Leave to stand for 10 minutes in a warm (not hot) place; the surface will become frothy. ❧ Sift the flour into a large mixing bowl with the salt. Make a well in the center and pour in the yeast liquid, the oil, and most of the remaining water. ❧ Stir with a wooden spoon until the flour has been absorbed. Add a little more warm water if necessary. ❧ Place the dough on a floured work surface and knead until it becomes very soft and elastic. ❧ Shape into a ball and place in a large bowl. Cover with a large clean cloth folded in half and leave to rise in a warm place, away from drafts, for 1 hour, or until the dough has doubled in volume. ❧ Knead the dough briefly on a lightly floured surface just before using. ❧ Heat the oil in a large skillet (frying pan) and sauté the garlic for 2–3 minutes. Remove the garlic and add the squid. Cook over a moderate heat, stirring frequently, for 15 minutes. ❧ Stir in the other ingredients and cook for 5 minutes. Season with salt and pepper. ❧ Divide the dough into two portions, one almost twice as large as the other. Roll the larger piece of dough out to a thickness of about $1/8$ in/3 mm. Use it to line the bottom and sides of a springform pan (tin). Leave enough dough to slightly overlap the edges. ❧ Fill the dough-lined springform pan with the squid mixture ❧ Roll out the smaller piece of dough to the same thickness as the first and use it to cover the springform pan. Fold the overlapping dough over the top to seal. ❧ Bake in a preheated oven at 400°F/200°C/gas 6 for 30 minutes. ❧ Serve hot or at room temperature.

*This unusual sweet and sour dish comes from Gaeta in southern Lazio, where the influence of Middle Eastern cooking is strongest.*

For the dough:
- 1 tablespoon/$1/2$ oz/15 g compressed/fresh baker's yeast or 3 teaspoons active dried yeast
- 1 teaspoon sugar
- about $3/4$ cup/6 fl oz/180 ml lukewarm water
- 3 cups/12 oz/350 g unbleached or all-purpose/strong plain flour, plus 2 tablespoons extra flour
- 1–2 teaspoons salt (to taste)
- $2^{1}/2$ tablespoons extra-virgin olive oil

For the filling:
- 4 tablespoons extra-virgin olive oil
- 1 clove garlic
- 14 oz/400 g squid (cleaned and prepared weight – ask your fish vendor to prepare it), coarsely chopped
- 4 ripe tomatoes, peeled and diced
- $1^{1}/2$ cups/7 oz/200 g pitted black olives
- 3 tablespoons golden raisins/sultanas
- 3 tablespoons pine nuts
- 3 tablespoons capers
- salt and pepper to taste

*Suggested wine: a dry, fruity white (Cerveteri Bianco)*

# Basic Recipes

For reasons of space I have moved a number of basic recipes to these pages. The Tomato Sauce is a classic and can be served with pasta, rice, potatoes, and in many other dishes. You can spice it up a little with a few slices of fresh chili pepper. The Clove-Flavored Meat Sauce (known as *Garofolato* in Italian) is an old Roman sauce; it is fairly time consuming and leaves you with a large piece of cooked meat as a by product, but do try it at least once – it has a quite unique flavor. I have included a recipe for Meat Broth; although a bouillon cube dissolved in boiling water will often suffice, some broth and pasta dishes do call for a homemade broth. Finally, I have included instructions for making fresh pasta at home.

### TOMATO SAUCE

Serves 4

2 cloves garlic, finely chopped

1 medium carrot, finely chopped

1 medium onion, finely chopped

1 stick celery, finely chopped

2 tablespoons finely chopped parsley

1/4 cup/2 fl oz/60 ml extra-virgin olive oil

2 cups/1 lb/500 g fresh or canned tomatoes, skinned and coarsely chopped

salt and freshly ground black pepper

6 fresh basil leaves, torn

Sauté the garlic, carrot, onion, celery, and parsley in the oil for 4–5 minutes. ✎ Add the tomatoes, season with salt and pepper and simmer uncovered over low heat for at least 45 minutes, or until the sauce has reduced to the required density. ✎ Turn off the heat, stir in the basil, and serve. ✎ For a spicy sauce, add chili peppers to taste. ✎ In late summer, when tomatoes are cheap and plentiful, make a large quantity in a very large, heavy-bottomed pan. Preserve in sterilized glass jars for use throughout the winter. When making large quantities of the sauce, simmer for at least 1 1/2 hours.

### CLOVE-FLAVORED MEAT SAUCE

Serves 6

1 1/2 lb/750 g topside veal

3 oz/90 g lard, chopped

2 cloves garlic, finely chopped

salt and freshly ground black pepper

8–10 cloves

1 medium carrot, finely chopped

1 stalk celery, finely chopped

1 small onion, finely chopped

2 tablespoons finely chopped parsley

1/2 cup/4 fl oz/125 ml dry white wine

1/2 cup/4 fl oz/125 ml canned tomatoes, coarsely chopped

Use a sharp knife to make 8–10 holes in the meat. Fill with half the lard and garlic, and salt and pepper. Press a clove into each filled hole. ✎ Tie the meat using kitchen string and place in a steep-sided pan. ✎ Sauté the remaining garlic in the rest of the lard with the carrot, celery, onion, and parsley for about 5 minutes. Add the vegetables and wine to the pan with the meat and cook over medium heat until the wine evaporates. ✎ Pour in the tomatoes and cover the meat with water. Partially cover the pan and cook until the sauce thickens (about 45 minutes). ✎ Use the sauce as directed in the recipes. The meat can be served separately as a main dish.

## MEAT BROTH

This broth freezes very well, so make a large quantity, pour it into small containers (ice cube trays are ideal) so that it can be used as required. Makes about 3 pints /1.5 liters.

2½ lb/1¼ kg various cuts beef with bones (neck, shoulder, short ribs, brisket)

2 carrots

2 onions

1 large stalk celery

2 ripe tomatoes

2 cloves garlic

2 sprigs parsley

1 bay leaf

5 pints/3 liters cold water

Put the meat, vegetables, and herbs into a large pot with the water. Cover and bring to the boil over medium heat. season with salt and pepper. ✒ Partially cover, and simmer over low heat for 3 hours. ✒ Turn off heat and leave to cool. ✒ When the broth is cool, remove the vegetables and herbs, and skim off and discard the fat that will have formed on top.

## MIXING PLAIN PASTA DOUGH

For 4 generous servings you will need 3½ cups/14 oz/400 g of all-purpose/plain flour and 4 medium eggs. Place the flour in a mound on a flat work surface and hollow out a well in the center. Break the eggs into the well one by one. Stir gently with a fork, gradually incorporating the flour. When the mixture is no longer runny, use your hands to finish combining the flour with the eggs. Work the mixture with your hands until it is smooth and moist, but quite firm.

To test the mixture for the correct consistency, press a clean finger into the dough. If it comes out without any dough sticking to it, it is ready for kneading. If it is too moist, add more flour. If it is too dry, incorporate a little milk. Roll the mixture into a ball shape.

## KNEADING THE DOUGH

Clean the work surface of any excess dough and lightly sprinkle with flour. Push down and forwards on the ball of pasta dough with the heel of your palm. Fold the slightly extended piece of dough in half, give it a quarter-turn, and repeat the process. Continue for about 10 minutes or until the dough is very smooth. Place the ball of pasta dough on a plate and cover with an upturned bowl. Leave to rest for at least 15–20 minutes.

## ROLLING THE DOUGH OUT BY HAND

Place the ball of dough on a flat, clean work surface and flatten it a little with your hand. Place the rolling pin on the center of the flattened ball and, applying light but firm pressure, roll the dough away from you. Give the ball a quarter-turn and repeat. When the dough has become a large round about ¼ in/5 mm thick, curl the far edge over the pin while holding the edge closest to you with your hand. Gently stretch the pasta as you roll it all onto the pin. Unroll, give the dough a quarter-turn, and repeat. Continue rolling and stretching the dough until it is transparent.

## ROLLING THE DOUGH OUT USING THE PASTA MACHINE

Divide the dough into several pieces and flatten them slightly with your hand. Set the machine with its rollers at their widest, and run each piece through the machine. Reduce the rollers' width by one notch and repeat, reducing the rollers' width by one notch each time. Continue until all the pieces have gone through the machine at the thinnest roller setting. Cut to the widths indicated in the recipes for tagliatelle and fettuccine.

# Gnocchi del Giovedì
## *Potato Dumplings*

Wash the potatoes thoroughly and cook in lightly salted boiling water with their skins on. ❧ Slip the skins off the cooked potatoes and mash them. Stir in the flour and salt. ❧ Beat the egg yolks with a fork until smooth. Add to the mixture and stir well until it is smooth. ❧ Take a handful of the mixture and roll it out on a lightly floured work surface using your hands. It should form a long sausage, about ¹/₂ in/1 cm in diameter. Use a sharp knife to cut the sausage into ³/₄-in/2-cm lengths. Repeat until all the mixture is used up. Place the little dumplings on a clean cloth to dry. Leave for at least 1 hour before cooking. ❧ Bring a large pot of salted water to a boil and add the dumplings in batches of about 30–40. When the dumplings have risen to the top, leave to bob around for about 2 minutes, then remove with a slotted spoon and place in a deep-sided serving bowl. Keep warm. Continue until all the dumplings are cooked. ❧ Pour the melted butter over the top and sprinkle with the parmesan. ❧ Serve at once.

*Serves 4–6*

*Preparation: 20 minutes + 1 hour's resting*

*Cooking: 25 minutes*

*Recipe grading: fairly easy*

- 3 lb/1.5 kg potatoes
- salt to taste
- 1 cup/4 oz/125 g all-purpose/plain flour
- 2 egg yolks
- 1 stick/4 oz/125 g butter, melted
- 1 cup/4 oz/125 g freshly grated parmesan cheese, plus more parmesan to serve separately at the table

*Suggested wine: a dry white (Frascati)*

*These little dumplings are served all over Italy. In Rome they are known as "Thursday's Dumplings" because they almost always appear on the menu on Thursday. Nobody quite knows why. For a more flavorsome sauce, add 6–8 leaves of fresh sage to the butter as you melt it.*

# Gnocchi alla Romana

*Baked Semolino Gnocchi*

*Serves 4*
*Preparation: 10 minutes*
*Cooking: 1 hour*
*Recipe grading: fairly easy*

- 4$\frac{1}{4}$ cups/1$\frac{3}{4}$ pints/1 liter milk
- 1$\frac{2}{3}$ cups/8 oz/250 g semolina
- salt to taste
- 1 stick/4 oz/125 g butter
- 2 egg yolks
- 1 cup/4 oz/125 g freshly grated parmesan cheese, plus more parmesan to serve separately at the table
- 1 tablespoon grated gruyère cheese
- freshly ground white pepper

*Suggested wine: a light, dry rosato*
*(Frusinate Rosato)*

*This delicious dish is known throughout Italy as "Gnocchi Roman-Style," even though it probably originated in Piedmont in the north. Children usually like gnocchi very much, so they are particularly suitable for a family meal.*

Bring the milk to a boil in a large, heavy-bottomed saucepan. ✺ Sprinkle the semolina in little by little, stirring all the time so that no lumps form. Keep stirring energetically for about 30 minutes, or until the mixture is dense. ✺ Remove from the heat and season with salt. Stir in half the butter, the egg yolks, half the parmesan, and the gruyère. ✺ Spread the mixture out to a thickness of about $\frac{1}{2}$ in/1 cm on a flat, lightly floured work surface. Leave to cool. ✺ Use a glass to cut discs of the mixture. Butter an ovenproof dish and use the pieces leftover after cutting out the disks to form a first layer in the dish. Sprinkle with a little of the remaining parmesan. Lay the disks over the top, one overlapping the next. ✺ Melt the remaining butter and pour over the top. Sprinkle with the remaining parmesan and a grinding of pepper. ✺ Bake in a preheated oven at 350°F/180°C/gas 4 for about 30 minutes. The gnocchi should be a lovely golden color. ✺ Serve hot.

# Penne alla Ricotta

*Penne with Ricotta Cheese*

Warm the milk and place in a bowl with the ricotta, sugar, cinnamon, and a dash of salt and white pepper. Mix with a fork to form a smooth, creamy sauce. ❧ Cook the penne in a large pot of salted, boiling water until *al dente*. Drain well and place in a heated serving bowl. Toss with the sauce and serve.

*Serves 4*
*Preparation: 5 minutes*
*Cooking: about 10 minutes*
*Recipe grading: easy*

- $^3/_4$ cups/6 fl oz/180 ml whole/full cream milk
- 8 oz/250 g very fresh ricotta cheese
- 1 tablespoon sugar
- 1 teaspoon ground cinnamon
- salt to taste
- freshly ground white pepper
- 1 lb/500 g penne

*Suggested wine: a dry, fruity white*
  *(Colli Albani Secco)*

*This classic southern Italian recipe is very simple and relies on the quality and freshness of the ricotta. Buy it loose from a specialty store or a good Italian deli. It is also good with fresh pasta.*

# Zuppa di Fave

*Fava Bean Soup*

Place the beans in a bowl and cover with cold water. Leave to soak for 12 hours. ❧ Drain the beans and cook in a pot of salted water for about 1 hour, or until they are tender. ❧ Heat the oil in a large heavy-bottomed pot (preferably earthenware) and sauté the pancetta, onion, celery, carrot, and marjoram (or parsley) until soft. ❧ Add the tomatoes and cook over a medium heat for 15 minutes. ❧ Add the prosciutto and cook for 2–3 minutes. ❧ Season with salt and pepper, then add the beans and 1 cup/8 fl oz /250 ml of boiling water. Cook for 10 minutes, stirring frequently. ❧ Toast the bread and place a half slice in the bottom of 4 individual soup plates. Ladle the soup over the top and serve hot.

*Serves 4*

*Preparation: 10 minutes + 12 hours' soaking*

*Cooking: about $1^3/4$ hours*

*Recipe grading: fairly easy*

- $1^3/4$ cups/12 oz/350 g dried fava beans/broad beans
- salt to taste
- 4 tablespoons extra-virgin olive oil
- $1/4$ cup/2 oz/60 g pancetta, diced
- 1 small onion, finely chopped
- 1 stalk celery, finely chopped
- 1 carrot, finely chopped
- 2 tablespoons finely chopped fresh marjoram (or parsley)
- $1^1/3$ cups/7 oz/200 g peeled and chopped fresh or canned tomatoes
- 4 oz/125 g prosciutto, diced
- 2 large, thick slices day-old bread
- freshly ground black pepper

*Suggested wine: a young dry red (Frascati Rosso)*

# Stracciatella alla Romana
## *Meat Broth with Egg*

*Serves 4*

*Preparation: 5 minutes + time to make the broth*

*Cooking: 30 minutes*

*Recipe grading: easy*

- 6¹/₂ cups/2¹/₂ pints/1.5 liters homemade meat broth (see recipe, page 49)
- 5 eggs
- salt to taste
- dash of grated nutmeg
- 4 tablespoons freshly grated parmesan cheese, plus more parmesan to serve separately at the table

*Suggested wine: a light, dry white (Castelli Romani)*

Prepare the broth (or reheat it, if using frozen broth). ❧ Beat the eggs with a dash each of salt and nutmeg. Add the 4 tablespoons of parmesan and beat until smooth. ❧ When the broth is boiling, pour in the egg mixture. Beat with a fork for 3–4 minutes over a medium heat until the egg begins to cook and has formed lots of tiny lumps. ❧ Serve at once, with abundant parmesan on hand to pass around separately.

*This simple, sustaining dish makes an excellent first course before serving boiled or roast meats.*

# Minestra di Broccoli

## *Broccoli and Tagliatelle Soup*

Wash the broccoli and trim the tough parts off the stalk. Dice the stalk and divide the tops into florets. ❧ Heat the oil in a large deep-sided pot and sauté the pork fat, garlic, and parsley for 4–5 minutes. ❧ Add the broccoli and cook for about 5 minutes, then add the tomato paste and water. Season with salt and pepper, then partially cover and cook a over medium-low heat for about 15 minutes, or until the broccoli is almost cooked. ❧ Add the tagliatelle and cook until it is *al dente*. ❧ Turn off the heat and leave for 3–4 minutes ❧ Serve hot with the parmesan passed around separately.

*Serves 4*
*Preparation: 10 minutes*
*Cooking: 25 minutes*
*Recipe grading: easy*

- 1 lb/500 g broccoli
- 2 tablespoons extra-virgin olive oil
- $^3/_4$ cup/3 oz/90 g pork fat, diced
- 2 cloves garlic, finely chopped
- 2 tablespoons finely chopped flat-leaf parsley
- 1 tablespoon concentrated tomato paste dissolved in $^1/_2$ cup/4 fl oz/125 ml warm water
- salt to taste
- 8 oz/250 g tagliatelle, broken or cut into pieces
- 6 tablespoons freshly grated parmesan cheese
- freshly ground black pepper

*Suggested wine: a light, dry white (Est! Est!! Est!!!)*

*A healthy winter soup that the whole family will love.*

# Secondi piatti

With over two million sheep in the region, it is not surprising that lamb is an important dish in Lazio. Roasted with rosemary and potatoes, broiled (grilled), or stewed – lamb appears on the menu every day in the trattorias of Rome. Chicken, pork, veal, and beef are also popular, usually cooked or served with vegetables, such as bell peppers or artichokes. The classic Mixed Fried Meat, Vegetables, and Bread combines them all, according to availability and the cook's tastes. Seafood is served along the coast, from the ancient Etruscan town of Civitavecchia in the north to Gaeta in the south. Seafood dishes based on mullet, bream, bass, sole, shrimp and prawns are among the most common.

# Pollo con Peperoni
## *Chicken with Bell Peppers*

Wash the chicken and pat it dry with a clean cloth. Cut into 8 pieces. ❧ Sauté the garlic in 2 tablespoons of the oil for 2–3 minutes, then add the tomatoes. Season with salt and pepper and cook over a moderate heat for 15 minutes, or until the sauce reduces. ❧ Clean the bell peppers, removing the seeds and core. Cut in quarters and place under the broiler (grill) until the skin blackens. Peel the blackened skin away with your fingers. Rinse the peppers and pat them dry. Cut into thin strips. ❧ Sauté the chicken in the remaining oil. Season with salt and pepper, then pour in the wine. Cook over a moderate heat for 15 minutes. ❧ Add the tomato sauce and the bell peppers and cook together for 10 minutes more. ❧ Serve hot.

*Serves 4*
*Preparation: 10 minutes*
*Cooking: 45 minutes*
*Recipe grading: fairly easy*

- 1 chicken, weighing about 2 lb/1 kg, cleaned
- 3 cloves garlic, finely chopped
- 8 tablespoons extra-virgin olive oil
- 2¹⁄₂ cups/14 oz/400 g peeled and chopped canned or fresh tomatoes
- salt to taste
- 1 lb/500 g bell peppers/capsicums, mixed green, yellow, and red
- scant 1 cup/7 fl oz/200 ml dry white wine
- freshly ground black pepper

*Suggested wine: a light, dry rosé (Sangiovese di Aprilia)*

*This dish is made throughout the summer and early fall, when bell peppers are at their tastiest and most plentiful. Try adding 1¹⁄₂ cups/ 7 oz /200 g of pitted whole black olives for even more flavor. The best black Gaeta olives are particularly recommended.*

# Saltimbocca alla Romana
*Braised Veal and Prosciutto Slices*

*Serves 4*
*Preparation: 10 minutes*
*Cooking: 5–6 minutes*
*Recipe grading: easy*

- 8 thin slices of veal, weighing about 1 lb/500 g in total
- 8 fresh sage leaves
- 4 thin slices of prosciutto, weighing about 3½ oz/100 g in total, cut in half
- ½ stick/2 oz/60 g butter
- salt to taste
- freshly ground black pepper
- 4 tablespoons dry white wine

*Suggested wine: a dry red (Fiorano Rosso)*

Beat the veal gently with a meat pounder, taking care not to pierce it. ❧ Place a leaf of sage at the center of each slice and cover with half a slice of prosciutto. Attach them to the veal using a toothpick, in the same way as you would use a safety pin. ❧ Melt the butter in a skillet (frying pan) large enough to hold the veal slices in a single layer. Add the veal, season with salt and pepper, and cook over a fairly high heat until done on one side. Drizzle with the wine and turn. Cook until the other side is done too. This should take only 5–6 minutes, otherwise the meat will become tough. ❧ Transfer the veal slices to a heated serving dish. Boil the remaining cooking juices for 1 minute, then pour over the veal. ❧ Serve hot.

*Serve these tasty veal slices with potato purée and a green salad.*

# Salsicce con Broccoletti
*Spicy Sausages with Flowering Turnip Tops*

Serves 4
Preparation: 5 minutes
Cooking: 25 minutes
Recipe grading: easy

- 2 cloves garlic, finely chopped
- $1/2$ teaspoon crushed chili pepper (or 1 medium red fresh chili pepper, thinly sliced)
- 2 tablespoons extra-virgin olive oil
- 8 large Italian sausages
- $1^1/4$ lb/625 g flowering turnip tops (or broccoli, if preferred)
- salt to taste
- freshly ground black pepper

*Suggested wine: a dry white (Orvieto)*

Sauté the garlic and chili pepper in the oil in a large skillet (frying pan) over a moderate heat until pale gold. ❧ Add the sausages and brown all over pricking them here and there with the tongs of a fork to let some of the fat run out. ❧ Clean and wash the flowering turnip tops and add to the skillet. Season with salt and pepper. Cook for 20 minutes, or until the vegetables are tender, but not overcooked. Add a little water during cooking if the skillet dries out to much. ❧ Serve hot.

*Flowering turnip tops, known as "broccoletti" in Italian, are a common winter vegetable in Lazio. You may substitute with the same amount of broccoli.*

# Costolette a Scottadito

## *Broiled Lamb Chops*

*Serves 4*
*Preparation: 5 minutes*
*Cooking: 15 minutes*
*Recipe grading: easy*

Place the chops on a large plate and drizzle with the oil, if using. Sprinkle with salt and a generous grinding of pepper. ❧ Arrange the chops in a grill pan and place over high heat. Turn frequently until they are well-cooked all over. If you don't have a grill pan, arrange the chops on a wire tray and place under the broiler (grill). Turn frequently until they are done. ❧ Serve very hot.

- 1 kg lamb chops
- 2 tablespoons extra-virgin olive oil (optional)
- salt to taste
- freshly ground black pepper

*Suggested wine: a dry red*
*(Merlot d'Aprilia)*

*These chops are even more delicious when cooked over a barbecue. Their Italian name "scottadito", means "finger burners" and refers to the fact that they are best eaten with your fingers.*

# Abbacchio al Forno

## *Roast Lamb and Potatoes*

Place the lamb in an ovenproof dish large enough to hold the lamb and the potatoes. ➣ Use the point of a sharp knife to make small incisions in the meat and push the pieces of garlic in. Close the meat around it, so that its flavor will permeate the meat during cooking. Run your hand backward up two of the rosemary sprigs and sprinkle the leaves over the lamb. Tuck the remaining sprigs in around the meat. Drizzle with the oil. Sprinkle with salt and pepper to taste. ➣ Place in a preheated oven at 350°F/180°C/gas 4. ➣ Feel the potatoes and cut into large bite-sized chunks. Arrange them around the meat after it has been in the oven for about 20 minutes. ➣ The meat should take about 1 hour to cook, while the potatoes will need only about 40 minutes. Baste the meat with the cooking juices 2 or 3 times during roasting and turn the potatoes so that they are evenly browned. ➣ Serve hot.

*Serves 4*
*Preparation: 10 minutes*
*Cooking: 1 hour*
*Recipe grading: easy*

- shoulder of baby lamb (with some loin attached), weighing about $2^{1}/_{4}$ lb/1.2 kg
- 2 cloves garlic, peeled and cut in half
- 4–6 sprigs fresh rosemary
- 4 tablespoons extra-virgin olive oil
- salt to taste
- freshly ground black pepper
- 2 lb/1 kg roasting potatoes

*Suggested wine: a dry red*
*(Cerveteri Rosso )*

*Roast baby lamb with potatoes is a traditional dish at Easter in many parts of Italy.*

# Food in Ancient Rome

In recent years the "Mediterranean diet" has become popular all over the world as people search for a healthy, low-cholesterol style of eating which is also appetizing. The origins of the Italian diet stretch back over 2,500 years to ancient Rome. Although many ingredients of modern Italian cuisine (the ubiquitous tomato is the most notable example) had not yet arrived from America, the basic diet of olive oil, wine, cheese, grains, fish, fruit, vegetables, and limited amounts of meat, was already in place. The ancient Romans had also discovered the importance of ambience for felicitous dining. Roman villas all had a dining room (wealthy people's villas had summer and winter dining rooms) with three long couches placed along the walls on which eight to ten people could recline comfortably as they ate, drank, and conversed. An inscription on the wall of a house in Pompeii has instructions for good behavior at evening parties: *Do not cast lustful glances or make eyes at another man's wife* (from which we learn that women were not banned from these parties as they were among the ancient Greeks in Athens). *Do not be course in your conversation. Restrain yourself from getting angry or using offensive language. If you cannot do so, then go home.*

Grapes, figs, and dates were basic foods. Besides being made into wine, grapes were eaten fresh or dried for consumption out of season.

Liquids such as olive oil and wine were transported and stored in large terra-cotta (baked earth) amphorae. The special Roman fish sauce known as "garum" was also stored in these containers. Garum was made from fish guts, heavily salted and then allowed to ferment in large tanks. The resulting sauce (which must have been very tasty indeed!) was used to flavor stews and casseroles and many other dishes too.

The streets and markets of ancient Roman towns were lined with shops selling bread, meat, fresh fruit and vegetables, as well as shoes, sandals, cloth, and other necessities. The ancient model above shows the proprietor of a fruit and vegetable store offering onions, garlic, and other fresh vegetables to his customers.

Italian painter G.P. Panini caught the "Grand Tour" spirit of the times in the early 18th century with his real and imaginary views of Roman ruins.

Right: An ancient Roman stove.

Roman cooks used bronze and iron pots and containers to prepare their food. They also had ceramic and glass dishes for serving it. Roman artisans were very skillful as many of the numerous pieces of glassware that have survived show.

Opposite page: Ancient Roman glassware.

# Zuppa di Cozze
## *Mussel Soup*

*Serves 4*

*Preparation: 10 minutes (+ 30 minutes soaking, if necessary)*

*Cooking: 5 minutes*

*Recipe grading: easy*

- 3 lb/1.5 kg fresh mussels in shell
- 4 tablespoons extra-virgin olive oil
- 2 tablespoons finely chopped flat-leaf parsley
- 2 cloves garlic, finely chopped
- salt to taste
- freshly ground black pepper

*Suggested wine: a light, dry white (Marino Secco Superiore)*

Scrub the mussels well to remove their beards and rinse thoroughly under cold running water. If they appear to be holding a lot of sand, leave to soak in cold water for 30 minutes. ❧ Heat the oil in a large, deep-sided skillet (frying pan) and sauté the mussels until they are all open. Discard any that do not open. ❧ Sprinkle with the parsley and garlic, then season with salt and pepper and cook for 4–5 minutes more. ❧ Serve hot.

*This dish is simplicity itself. To succeed, be sure to buy the very freshest of mussels. Serve with firm-textured bread, toasted briefly in a hot oven and drizzled with the highest quality extra-virgin olive oil.*

# Baccalà con Peperoni
## *Salt Cod with Bell Peppers*

Skin the salt cod and remove the bones. Rinse under cold running water and pat dry with paper towels, then cut into pieces. ❧ Heat the frying oil in a large skillet (frying pan) until hot, but not smoking. Flour the salt cod then fry in the oil until cooked. Drain on paper towels and set aside in a warm place. ❧ Sauté the onion in the extra-virgin olive oil in a deep-sided skillet until transparent. ❧ Add the tomatoes and cook over a moderate heat for 15 minutes, or until the sauce reduces. Season with salt and pepper. ❧ Clean the bell peppers, removing the seeds and core. Cut into quarters and place under the broiler (grill) until the skin blackens. Peel the blackened skin away with your fingers. Rinse the bell peppers and pat them dry. Cut into thin strips. ❧ Add the bell peppers and salt cod to the skillet with the tomato sauce. Cook together for 5 minutes, then serve.

*Serves 4*
*Preparation: 10 minutes*
*Cooking: 25 minutes*
*Recipe grading: easy*

- $1^1/_2$ lb/750 g pre-soaked salt cod
- 1–2 cups/8–16 fl oz/250–500 ml olive oil for frying
- scant 1 cup/$3^1/_2$ oz/100 g all purpose/plain flour
- 1 large onion, finely chopped
- 4 tablespoons extra-virgin olive oil
- 14 oz/400 g peeled and diced fresh or canned tomatoes
- 3 large bell peppers/capsicums, preferably 1 red, 1 yellow, 1 green
- salt to taste
- freshly ground black pepper

*Suggested wine: a dry white (Cerveteri Bianco)*

*Salt cod, a typically northern European dish, is popular all over Italy. It was adopted centuries ago after trading contacts were made with Holland and Scandinavia. In Rome it is usually served with a sweet and sour sauce, with bell peppers, or fried in a simple egg and flour batter.*

# Stufatino

## *Roman-Style Beef Stew*

Heat the pork fat in a large, heavy-bottomed pan and sauté the onion. When the onion turns pale gold, add the oil, garlic, and celery and sauté for 5 minutes. ❧ Add the beef and season with salt and pepper. Stir continually until the meat is lightly browned all over. ❧ Pour in the wine and cook until it evaporates. Add the tomatoes and cook for another 10 minutes, stirring frequently. ❧ Add enough cold water to cover the meat. Cover and cook over a low heat for at least 2 hours. The sauce should be thick and dark in color. ❧ Remove from the heat and stir in the marjoram or parsley just before serving. ❧ Serve hot.

*Serves 4*
*Preparation: 10 minutes*
*Cooking: about 2¼ hours*
*Recipe grading: easy*

- ¼ cup/2 oz/60 g pork fat
- 1 large onion, finely chopped
- 2 tablespoons extra-virgin olive oil
- 2 cloves garlic, finely chopped
- 1 stalk celery, finely chopped
- 1 lb/500 g boneless beef chuck, cut into 1½-in/4-cm cubes
- scant ½ cup/3½ fl oz/100 ml dry white wine
- 2 large ripe tomatoes, peeled and diced
- salt to taste
- freshly ground black pepper
- 1 tablespoon finely chopped marjoram (or parsley)

*Suggested wine: a dry red*
*(Cerveteri Rosso )*

*To freshen the dish a little, it is traditional to add 1 cup/3½ oz/100 g of coarsely chopped, lightly boiled celery stalks to the pot 5 minutes before serving. The stew is particularly good and hearty when served with boiled potatoes cooked briefly in tomato sauce (see recipe, page 48).*

*Serves 4*

*Preparation: 15 minutes*

*Cooking: 1¹/₄ hours*

*Recipe grading: easy*

- 3 cloves garlic, finely chopped
- 1 tablespoon finely chopped rosemary leaves
- 4 sage leaves
- 4 tablespoons extra-virgin olive oil
- 2 lb/1 kg tender young lamb shoulder, cut into 2-in/5-cm cubes with the bone left in
- salt to taste
- freshly ground black pepper
- 1 tablespoon all-purpose/plain flour
- scant ¹/₂ cup/3¹/₂ fl oz/100 ml white wine vinegar
- 4 tablespoons cold water
- 6 anchovy fillets

*Suggested wine: a dry red (Merlot d'Aprilia)*

# Abbacchio alla Romana
## *Roman-Style Braised Lamb*

Sauté the garlic, rosemary, and sage in the oil in a large, deep-sided skillet (frying pan). ❧ Add the lamb and season with salt and pepper. Stir in the flour, vinegar, and water. Cover and cook over a low heat for 1 hour, adding extra water if the cooking liquid dries out too much. ❧ Put 2 tablespoons of the cooking liquid in a small bowl and dissolve the anchovy fillets in it. Pour back into the stew and stir well. ❧ Cook for another 2–3 minutes, then remove from the heat and serve.

*This is one of the classics of Roman cooking. It goes well with many vegetables, including boiled potatoes, or Peas with Ham Roman-Style (see recipe, page 85), and Mixed Braised Bell Peppers (see recipe, page 92).*

# Pollo con Verdure

## *Braised Chicken and Vegetables*

Sauté the onion and garlic (if using) in the oil in a large, deep-sided skillet (frying pan) until they turn pale gold. ✑ Add the chicken and brown all over. ✑ Pour in the wine and cook until it evaporates. Add the potatoes, carrots, celery, and parsley and season with salt and pepper. ✑ Pour in enough broth to moisten the dish, then cover and cook over a moderate heat for 25–30 minutes, stirring frequently. Add more broth as required during cooking. ✑ When the chicken is cooked and the vegetables tender, remove from the heat and serve.

*Serves 4*
*Preparation: 10 minutes*
*Cooking: 35 minutes*
*Recipe grading: easy*

- 1 large onion, finely chopped
- 2 cloves garlic, finely chopped (optional)
- 4 tablespoons extra-virgin olive oil
- 1 chicken, weighing about 3 lb/1.5 kg, cut into 8 pieces
- $^1/_2$ cup/4 fl oz/125 ml dry white wine
- 14 oz/400 g potatoes, peeled and coarsely chopped
- 4 medium carrots, peeled and coarsely chopped
- 2 stalks celery, coarsely chopped
- 2 tablespoons finely chopped parsley
- $^2/_3$ cup/5 fl oz/150 ml chicken or vegetable broth (homemade or bouillon cube)
- salt to taste
- freshly ground black pepper

*Suggested wine: a dry white (Orvieto)*

# Lamb – a Roman Staple

The ancient Romans preferred kid (young goat's meat) over lamb; modern Romans have inverted this preference and lamb is now the most typical meat dish served. Known in the local dialect as "*abbacchio*" (from the verbs *abbacchiare* or *abbattere,* which mean "to butcher"), traditionally the most highly-prized lamb had to be less than a month old and still be fed on its mother's milk. Recently this very strict definition has been stretched a little and slightly older, weaned lambs are also served as *abbacchio.* Although fresh lamb is now available throughout the year, spring is the best season for it. *Abbacchio* is perhaps the most typical dish for Easter meals. Distinguishing real *abbacchio* from mature meat is an art: it is not sufficient to check that the weight corresponds to the age of the animal – the meat itself has to be a very pale pink color. Darker meat raises doubts about the real age of the lamb. *Abbacchio* can be grilled, braised, roasted, or fried and is often served with potatoes. The lamb and artichoke recipe below combines two classic ingredients of Roman cooking.

**LAMB WITH ARTICHOKES**
Serves 4

*4 large artichokes*
*juice of 1 lemon*
*2 oz/60 g prosciutto*
*2 cloves garlic*
*small bunch of parsley or marjoram*
*2 lbs/1 kg lamb chops*
*1 small onion, finely chopped*
*½ cup/4 fl oz/125 ml dry white wine*
*1 tablespoon tomato paste*
*salt and freshly ground black pepper to taste*

Clean the artichokes as explained on page 90. Cut them in quarters and place in a bowl of cold water with the lemon juice. ❧ Finely chop the prosciutto, garlic, and parsley together and transfer to a large skillet (frying pan). Sauté for 3–4 minutes, then add the lamb chops and onion. Season with salt and pepper. ❧ When the onion is transparent, pour in the wine and cook until it has evaporated. ❧ Add the tomato paste and the drained artichokes. Cover, and cook over medium-low heat for about 15–20 minutes, or until the lamb and artichokes are tender. ❧ Serve hot.

The citizens of Rome have always been great lovers of lamb and all kinds of meat. Records from 1598 show that 73,000 lambs, 14,400 cows, 12,000 calves, 22,800 steers, 20,000 pigs, 818 piglets, and 600 oxen were officially butchered in the city during that year! The detailed records show the very strict control kept by city authorities.

The lamb is associated with Rome in more ways than one. The shepherd and the lamb are both traditional symbols of Christianity, and Rome has been the capital of Western Christendom for almost 2,000 years.

Lamb is usually butchered into three main parts called the "coscia" (leg), "spalla" (shoulder) and "lombata" (loin).

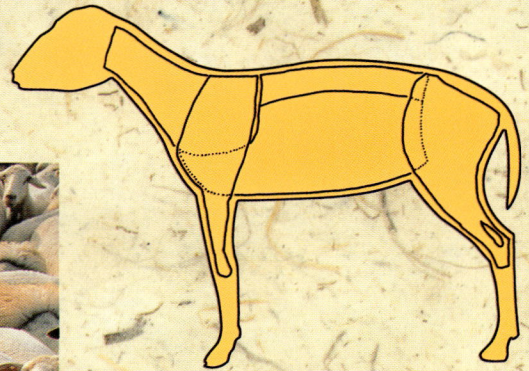

Nowadays there are over two million sheep in Lazio – Sardinia is the only Italian region with more of these animals.

# Fritto Misto

*Mixed Fried Meat, Vegetables, and Bread*

*Serves 4*
*Preparation: 20 minutes*
*Cooking: 30 minutes*
*Recipe grading: fairly easy*

- 1 calf's brain, about 1 lb/500 g
- 1 lb/500 g calf's liver, cut in slices $^{1}/_{2}$ in/1 cm thick
- 4–6 globe artichokes
- juice of 1 lemon
- 4–8 slices firm-textured bread
- about 4 tablespoons milk
- 1–2 cups/8–16 fl oz/250–500 ml olive oil for frying
- 1$^{1}/_{4}$ cups/5 oz/150 g all-purpose/ plain flour
- 3 eggs, beaten
- salt to taste

*Suggested wine: a dry red*
*(Sangiovese d'Aprilia)*

Wash the calf's brains thoroughly under cold running water, then soak in a bowl of cold water for 10 minutes. ⌘ Place in a pot of cold water and boil for 20 minutes. Remove all the brown parts and cut the brain into 6 pieces. ⌘ Cut the calf's liver into pieces about 1$^{1}/_{4}$ x 1$^{1}/_{2}$ in/3 x 4 cm. ⌘ Clean the artichokes by trimming the tops and stalk (leave about $^{1}/_{4}$ in/1 cm of stalk attached). Remove all the tough outer leaves so that only the pale, inner part remains. Cut each artichoke into quarters. As you clean the artichokes, place them in a large bowl of cold water with the lemon juice (this will stop them from discoloring). Drain well and pat dry. ⌘ Place the bread on a plate and drizzle with the milk. The slices should be damp, but not soggy. ⌘ Heat the oil in a deep-sided skillet (frying pan) until hot, but not smoking. ⌘ Dip the meats, artichokes, and bread in the flour, then in the egg. Fry in the oil, turning frequently, until golden brown all over. Drain on paper towels. Don't try to fry too much at once. The pieces of meat and artichokes should not touch one another. ⌘ Sprinkle with salt and serve immediately.

*These are the three most traditional ingredients in a Roman Fritto Misto, but you can use many others as well. Most meats fry well, as do vegetables. Onions, cauliflower, and zucchini (courgettes) are particularly suitable. The wonderful crisp fried bread is known as "pandorato" – "golden bread" – in Rome.*

# Trippa alla Trasteverina

## *Baked Tripe Trastevere-Style*

Heat the oil in a skillet (frying pan) and add the carrot, onion, celery, and garlic. Sauté for 5 minutes, then add the tomatoes. Sauté over a medium heat for 5–10 minutes more. ❧ Cut the tripe into large diamond shapes. ❧ Pour a little of the sauce into the bottom of a deep-sided ovenproof dish and cover with a layer of tripe. Sprinkle with some of the cheese and mint. Repeat this process until all the ingredients are used up. Make sure you finish with a layer of cheese. ❧ Bake in a preheated oven at 350°F/180°C/gas 4 for 30 minutes. ❧ Serve hot with a little extra cheese and mint sprinkled over the top, if liked.

*Serves 4*
*Preparation: 10 minutes*
*Cooking: 40 minutes*
*Recipe grading: easy*

- 4 tablespoons extra-virgin olive oil
- 1 carrot, finely chopped
- 1 onion, finely chopped
- 1 stalk celery, finely chopped
- 2 cloves garlic, finely chopped
- $1/4$ cup/2 oz/60 g peeled and diced, fresh or tinned tomatoes
- 2 lb/1 kg ready-to-cook, calf's honeycomb tripe
- $1^1/4$ cups/5 oz/150 g freshly grated pecorino romano cheese
- 8–10 fresh mint leaves, torn

*Suggested wine: a light, dry red*
*(Genazzano Rosso)*

*The traditional recipe calls for the rather special Clove-Flavored Meat Sauce (see recipe, page 49). Because you may not always have this on hand, we have given a modern, easy-to-make recipe for the sauce.*

# Frittata alla Ciociara
*Frosinone Omelet*

*Serves 2–4*
*Preparation: 5 minutes*
*Cooking: 10 minutes*
*Recipe grading: easy*

- 6 large eggs
- 2 tablespoons/1 oz/30 g pancetta, cut into small dice
- 2 tablespoons/1 oz/30 g mozzarella cheese, cut into small dice
- 1 tablespoon finely chopped shallots
- ½ stick/2 oz/60 g butter
- salt to taste
- freshly ground black pepper

*Suggested wine: a dry rosé*
*(Viganello Rosato)*

Combine the eggs, pancetta, mozzarella, shallots, salt, and pepper in a mixing bowl. ❧ Heat two-thirds of the butter over a moderate heat in a medium-sized skillet (frying pan) until it turns light gold. Pour in the egg mixture and stir for a few seconds. Cook until golden brown underneath. Turn the half-cooked omelet out onto a large plate. ❧ Add the remaining butter to the skillet. When it turns gold, return the omelet to the skillet with the other side underneath and cook until golden brown. ❧ When the egg is cooked (dry, but not overcooked), slip the omelet onto a heated dish and serve at once.

*Easy to prepare and tasty, Frosinone omelet makes an excellent light lunch. Serve it with a green salad.*

# Fish

The Tyrrhenian Sea that washes the shores of Lazio is teeming with seafood of every kind. The city of Rome gets its fish fresh every morning from the tiny port of Fiumicino on the coast. By lunchtime many of the bustling restaurants of the capital have a good selection of seafood dishes on their menus. This is a relatively new development, since fish were not so popular in Rome until around 50 years ago. Up until then they were mostly served in the homes of the aristocracy or in convents and other Christian places where the consumption of meat was limited for religious reasons. The advent of refrigeration and more efficient transportation after World War II made seafood available for people who lived inland. The coastal villages and towns, from Civitavecchia in the north to Gaeta in the south, have always relied on the sea and fish is an important part of the coastal diet and culinary traditions.

*Local fishermen ply the coastal waters with their nets in the early hours of the morning. The water is fairly clean and the quality of the catch is generally excellent. This is not so in the Tiber River that runs through Rome, which is very polluted. Although there are still many fish in the river and fishing competitions are common along its banks, the fish themselves are not fit for human consumption.*

Molluscs and crustaceans, including shrimp, calamari, octopus, clams, and mussels, are known collectively as "frutti di mare" (fruits of the sea) in Italian. They are often cooked quickly in a pan or grill and served with a simple dressing made with extra-virgin olive oil, garlic, parsley, and salt and pepper. This method is only successful if using the freshest seafood. Frozen frutti di mare are not recommended in this case.

Untangling the nets after a successful morning's fishing.

Beautiful Lake Bolsena has trout, pike, tench, whitefish, mullet, and eels to offer the inhabitants of the surrounding villages. These fish are prepared in a wide variety of ways: fettuccine pasta with peas cooked in tench broth is one of the most typical (and delicious!) local dishes.

# Verdure

Globe artichokes are the emblematic vegetable in Roman cooking. When you step into a trattoria during the season (from October until May), you will see them raw, piled high on platters, or cooked, stem up in earthenware dishes, in the classic Roman style. Artichokes. There are many varieties, but the plump Roman artichoke is the most common. Beyond the sprawling suburbs of the capital, Lazio is a primarily an agricultural region and a large variety of vegetables are produced throughout the year. Crisp romaine lettuce is widely cultivated, as are bell peppers, green beans, peas, and sweet baby onions. Gathered in the afternoon and sold early next morning in Rome, the overall quality is excellent because they are so fresh.

# Piselli alla Romana

## *Peas with Ham, Roman-Style*

*Serves 4*
*Preparation: 5 minutes*
*Cooking: about 10 minutes*
*Recipe grading: easy*

Sauté the onion in the lard (or butter) over a medium heat until it turns pale gold. ❧ Add the peas and broth. Season with salt and pepper and cook for 10 minutes, or until the peas are tender. ❧ Add the prosciutto 2 minutes before the peas are cooked. ❧ Serve hot.

- 1 small onion, finely chopped
- $1/2$ stick/2 oz/60 g lard (or butter)
- $1^1/_2$ lb/750 g fresh shelled (or frozen) sweet young peas
- scant $1/2$ cup/$3^1/_2$ fl oz/100 ml meat broth (homemade or bouillon cube)
- salt to taste
- freshly ground black pepper
- 3 oz/90 g prosciutto, cut in one thick slice, then diced

*Suggested wine: a dry white*
*(Frascati Novello)*

*This is a classic Roman side dish. The peas from the region of Lazio are small and sweet. You may need to add a dash of sugar if you are using larger, tougher peas.*

*Serves 4*
*Preparation: 10 minutes*
*Cooking: 20 minutes*
*Recipe grading: easy*

- 8 large globe artichokes
- juice of 1 lemon
- 1 cup/8 fl oz/250 ml extra-virgin olive oil
- salt to taste

*Suggested wine: a dry red
(Colli Albani)*

# Carciofi alla Giudia
## *Jewish-Style Artichokes*

Clean the artichokes by trimming the tops and stalk (leave about $1^1/_2$ in/4 cm of stalk attached). Remove all the tough outer leaves so that only the pale, inner part remains. As you clean the artichokes, place them in a large bowl of cold water with the lemon juice (this will stop them from discoloring). ❧ Drain and bang each artichoke down on the bench so that the leaves open out a little. ❧ Heat the oil in a large skillet (frying pan) and add the artichokes. Cook for about 15–20 minutes over a medium heat. When the artichokes are tender, turn up the heat and brown them for 2–3 minutes. They should turn a lovely golden brown at this stage. ❧ Drain on paper towels, sprinkle with salt, and serve at once.

*Artichokes are a staple vegetable in Rome during the winter months and are prepared in myriad ways. This is one of the heartiest dishes.*

# Eating in Rome

Romans love to eat out and the city is packed with cafés, *enoteche* (wine bars), pizzerias, pubs, trattorias, and restaurants. With only a little effort at getting off the beaten track, visitors can sample the delights of Roman cooking alongside the locals. With the exception of the Chinese restaurants that have mushroomed over the last decade, most eateries offer Roman food, or specialties from other regions of Italy. The quality is generally very high and the prices more than reasonable. The *enoteche* or wine bars that now dot the streets of Rome are a relatively new addition to the culinary cityscape and are really worth a try. Here you can get smallish servings of hot or cold dishes served with an excellent glass of wine. These places have sprung up in the last 20 to 30 years as daily lunchtimes have dwindled from three hour siestas to 30 minute breaks. The food served is generally excellent and the choice and quality of the wines usually impeccable. The more informal surroundings attract a younger, wealthier, and less traditional clientele.

"When in Rome, do as the Romans do" – particularly at breakfast time. This means you can start the day with a variety of pastries and a delicious cappuccino.

There is nothing new about dining out in Rome; the locals have been at it for over 2,000 years. The painting (top left) shows the doorway of a trattoria serving Castelli wine during the 18th century. The larger one (left), shows a scene in a typical restaurant in the 19th century.

Romans know that fresh, high quality ingredients are the key to good cooking and excellent food. Even crowded, expensive, central Rome has its street markets so that the locals can buy what they need. Campo de' Fiori is certainly the largest and probably the most beautiful of them all. Every morning except Sunday, the old piazza bustles with stalls selling fruit, vegetables, fish, cheeses, and other produce. Nearby delicatessens and bakeries offer excellent bread and other specialties.

No visit to Rome would be complete without sampling a porchetta (roast pork) sandwich or roll. Whole pigs are stuffed with salt and spices and then cooked. Thick slices of pork between two slabs of bread make a hearty lunch or snack.

*Serves 4*
*Preparation: 10 minutes*
*Cooking: 35 minutes*
*Recipe grading: easy*

- 8 medium artichokes
- juice of 1 lemon
- 1 onion, finely chopped
- 2 tablespoons extra-virgin olive oil
- $1/4$ cup/2 oz/60 g prosciutto, chopped
- salt to taste
- freshly ground black pepper
- 12 oz/350 g fresh shelled (or frozen) peas

*Suggested wine: a dry red (Castelli Romani)*

# Carciofi con Piselli

*Artichokes and Peas*

Clean the artichokes by trimming the tops and stalk. Remove all the tough outer leaves so that only the pale, inner part remains. Cut each artichoke in half and place in a large bowl of cold water with the lemon juice (this will stop them from discoloring). ❧ Sauté the onion in the oil in a large skillet (frying pan) until pale gold. Add the prosciutto. ❧ Drain the artichokes and add them to the skillet. Cook for 10 minutes, or until they are tender ❧ Season with salt and pepper and add the peas. Cook over medium heat for about 15–20 minutes, or until the peas and artichokes are both tender Add a little cold water as necessary to keep the vegetables moist. ❧ Serve hot or at room temperature.

*The peas and artichokes together make a rich and nourishing dish. This recipe is ideal for vegetarians and can be served, with bread and salad, as a light lunch.*

# Melanzane Ripiene

## *Stuffed Eggplants*

Serves 4
Preparation: 20 minutes
Cooking: 30 minutes
Recipe grading: easy

Rinse the eggplants thoroughly under cold running water and slice them in half. Use a sharp knife to hollow out the flesh, taking care not to pierce the skins. ❧ Dice the eggplant flesh and combine with the mozzarella and garlic (if using). Drizzle with 2 tablespoons of the oil and season with salt and pepper. Mix well. ❧ Arrange the hollowed-out eggplant halves in a shallow, ovenproof dish. Fill with the mozzarella mixture. Spoon the chopped tomato over the top. ❧ Bake in a preheated oven at 350°F/180°C/gas 4 for about 30 minutes. ❧ Serve hot or at room temperature.

- 4 small eggplants/aubergines
- 8 oz/250 g mozzarella cheese, cut into $\frac{1}{2}$ in/1 cm dice
- 1 clove garlic, finely chopped (optional)
- 3 tablespoons extra-virgin olive oil
- salt to taste
- freshly ground black pepper
- 3 large ripe tomatoes, peeled and diced

*Suggested wine: a dry white*
*(Cerveteri Bianco)*

*These eggplants are so simple to prepare yet they are always a success. Serve them as a side dish or an appetizer. Add a few torn basil leaves to the tomato mixture for extra flavor.*

# Peperonata

## *Mixed Braised Bell Peppers*

*Serves 4–6*
*Preparation: 10 minutes*
*Cooking: 25 minutes*
*Recipe grading: easy*

- 4–6 bell peppers/capsicums (mixed red, green, and yellow), cut into $1/2$-in/1-cm strips
- 2 large onions, thinly sliced
- $3^1/4$ cups/1 lb/500 g peeled and chopped fresh or canned tomatoes
- 4 tablespoons extra-virgin olive oil
- 3 cloves garlic, finely chopped
- salt to taste
- freshly ground black pepper
- 6 leaves fresh basil, torn

*Suggested wine: a light, dry white (Frascati)*

Place the vegetables in a large heavy-bottomed saucepan or earthenware pot. Add the oil and garlic, and season with salt and pepper. Cover and cook over a medium heat for about 15 minutes. ❧ Turn the heat up to high and partially uncover to let some of the liquid evaporate. Cook until the bell peppers are tender. ❧ Garnish with basil leaves and serve hot or at room temperature.

*This classic dish is delicious when cooked in an earthenware pot. For a stronger, more distinctive flavor, add 1 medium eggplant (aubergine), diced but not peeled, 1 cup/5 oz/ 150 g of pitted black olives, and 1 teaspoon of oregano.*

*Serves 4*
*Preparation: 20 minutes*
*Cooking: 30 minutes*
*Recipe grading: easy*

- 1¼ lb/625 g fresh or 14 oz/400 g frozen spinach
- salt to taste
- 7 oz/200 g ricotta cheese
- 2 tablespoons all-purpose/plain flour plus extra for flouring
- 2 eggs
- freshly ground black pepper
- 1 cup/8 fl oz/250 ml olive oil for frying

*Suggested wine: a dry white (Colli Albani)*

# Polpette di Spinaci e Ricotta
## *Spinach and Ricotta Croquettes*

If using fresh spinach, trim the stalks and rinse well under cold running water. ❧ Place the spinach in a small pan of salted water and cook over a medium high heat for 7–10 minutes, or until tender. ❧ Drain well and squeeze out all the excess moisture. Transfer to a chopping board and chop finely. ❧ Combine the spinach in a bowl with the ricotta, flour, eggs, salt, and pepper and mix well. ❧ Heat the oil in a skillet (frying pan) until very hot, but not smoking. ❧ Shape spoonfuls of the spinach mixture into walnut-sized balls and roll them in the extra flour. ❧ Fry the croquettes in the oil, turning them frequently, until they are crisp and well-cooked. ❧ Drain on paper towels, then sprinkle with a little salt and serve at once.

# Zucchine Marinate
## *Marinated Zucchini*

Wash the zucchini under cold running water and trim the ends off. Dry well with paper towels. Cut the zucchini into wheels. ❧ Heat the oil in a large skillet (frying pan) and fry the zucchini wheels in 2 or 3 batches for 7–8 minutes. ❧ Place the cooked zucchini in a deep-sided dish. ❧ Heat the vinegar with the salt and chile pepper until it begins to boil. Pour over the zucchini. ❧ Season with a generous grinding of black pepper and cover. Set aside for 24 hours before use. ❧ Serve at room temperature.

*Serves 6*
*Preparation: 5 minutes*
*Cooking: 25 minutes*
*Recipe grading: easy*

- 8 large zucchini/courgettes
- 4 tablespoons extra-virgin olive oil
- 1 cup/8 fl oz/250 ml white wine vinegar
- salt to taste
- 1 red chile pepper
- freshly ground black pepper

*Suggested wine: a light, dry white*
*(Est! Est!! Est!!!))*

*Serves 4*

*Preparation: 15 minutes + 20 minutes'*
*  resting*

*Cooking: about 20 minutes*

*Recipe grading: easy*

- 3 large potatoes
- salt to taste
- ¹/₂ medium Savoy cabbage
- 2 tablespoons extra-virgin olive oil
- 1 small onion, finely chopped
- ¹/₄ cup/2 oz/60 g pancetta, diced
- 1 clove garlic, finely chopped
- ¹/₂ teaspoon crushed chile pepper
- freshly ground black pepper

*Suggested wine: a light, dry white (Frascati)*

# Patate e Cavoli
## *Potato and Cabbage Mix*

Cook the potatoes in a large pot of salted, boiling water. Peel and mash them. ❧ Boil the cabbage in another pot of salted water for 10 minutes. Drain well and chop coarsely. ❧ Heat the oil in a large skillet (frying pan) and sauté the onion until pale gold. Add the pancetta, garlic, and chile pepper. Season with salt and pepper, then add the potatoes and cabbage. ❧ Mix well and then set aside for about 20 minutes to absorb the flavors. ❧ Serve warm or at room temperature.

*Serves 6*
*Preparation: 20 minutes*
*Cooking: 30 minutes*
*Recipe grading: easy*

- 14 oz/400 g porcini mushrooms
- 1 cup/8fl oz/250 ml olive oil for frying
- 1¼ cups/5 oz/150 g all-purpose/plain flour
- salt to taste

*Suggested wine: a dry white*
*(Colli Albani)*

# Funghi Dorati
*Fried Porcini Mushrooms*

Wash the mushrooms under cold running water and pat dry with paper towels. Trim off the roots and discard. Slice the stalks and heads. ❧ Heat the oil in a large skillet (frying pan) until very hot, but not smoking. ❧ Dip the mushrooms in the flour and then fry in the oil, turning frequently, until golden brown. ❧ Drain on paper towels and sprinkle with a little salt (if liked). ❧ Serve at once.

*Mouth-watering porcini mushrooms grow wild in the woods in Italy. Mushroom hunters wander in the woods after every shower of rain in spring or fall. If you can't get porcini, substitute another wild mushroom. You may need to fry for a little more or less time.*

Serves 4–6
Preparation: 10 minutes
Cooking: 35 minutes
Recipe grading: easy

# Cipolline in Agrodolce
## *Sweet and Sour Baby Onions*

Clean the onions and place them in a bowl of cold water. ❧ Sauté the prosciutto in the lard (or butter or oil). ❧ Drain the onions and add to the pan. Season with salt and pepper and add the sugar. Pour in the vinegar and water. ❧ Cook over a medium-low heat until the onions are tender and the cooking juices have almost all been absorbed. ❧ Serve hot or at room temperature.

- 1 lb/500 g white baby onions
- 1/4 cup/2 oz/60 g prosciutto, coarsely chopped
- 1 tablespoon lard (or butter or extra-virgin olive oil)
- salt to taste
- freshly ground black pepper
- 1 tablespoon sugar
- 3 tablespoons white wine vinegar
- scant 1/2 cup/3 1/2 fl oz/100 ml cold water

*Suggested wine: a light, dry white
(Colli Albani)*

# Dolci

Cakes, cookies, and desserts are less of a feature in Roman cooking than in many other regions of Italy. Cooks in the Eternal City have gladly adopted dishes from other regions and countries and a typical trattoria will offer a variety of dishes from other parts of Italy and abroad. However, there are a limited number of traditional dishes, usually linked to feast days or specific towns in Lazio, which are well worth trying. The Candied Fruit and Pine Nut Buns and Sweet Pizza from Civitavecchia are the two best examples of these. As in many other regions, fritters are always popular, and are also linked to seasons or feast days. Fresh Roman ricotta cheese is a basic ingredient in many desserts, above all in the very special Ricotta Cream.

# Fette di Mele Fritte

## *Sliced Apple Fritters*

*Serves 4–6*

*Preparation: 10 minutes + 1 hour's resting*

*Cooking: 15 minutes*

*Recipe grading: fairly easy*

Separate the eggs and beat the yolks in a bowl until smooth. ❧ Add the flour, wine, extra-virgin olive oil, and a dash of salt and mix to obtain a smooth, fairly liquid batter. Cover the bowl and set aside to rest for 1 hour. ❧ Peel and core the apples, leaving them whole. Slice crosswise and drizzle with the lemon juice to stop them turning black. ❧ Heat enough oil to cover the bottom of a large skillet (frying pan) until very hot, but not smoking. ❧ Beat the egg whites until they form stiff peaks. Stir into the batter. ❧ Dip the apple slices into the batter and fry in batches until light golden brown on both sides. Don't put too many slices in the pan at once or they will stick together. Repeat until all the apples are used up. ❧ Place the fried slices on paper towels to drain. Keep them on a warm plate as you finish the rest. ❧ Sprinkle with confectioners' sugar and serve immediately.

- 2 eggs
- 1 cup/4 oz/125 g all-purpose/plain flour
- $\frac{1}{2}$ cup/4 fl oz/125 ml dry white wine
- 2 tablespoons extra-virgin olive oil
- salt to taste
- 6 cooking apples
- juice of 1 lemon
- olive oil for frying
- confectioners'/icing sugar

*Suggested wine: a sweet white (Cesanese del Piglio Dolce)*

*Simple and elegant, this dessert goes very well with vanilla ice cream or whipped cream. Be sure to keep the apples hot until you serve them. Ideally, they should be served as soon after cooking as possible.*

# Maritozzi
## *Candied Fruit and Pine Nut Buns*

Crumble the yeast into a small bowl with 5 tablespoons of the water, stirring until the yeast dissolves. ❧ Leave to stand for 10 minutes in a warm (not hot) place until the surface is frothy. ❧ Place about one-third of the flour in a mixing bowl and stir in the yeast mixture. Transfer the dough to a floured work surface and knead to obtain a smooth dough. Cover with a clean cloth and set aside to rise for about 3 hours. ❧ Transfer the risen dough to a lightly floured work surface and knead in the remaining flour, the oil, sugar, golden raisins, pine nuts, candied fruit, and a dash of salt. Add the remaining water as required to obtain a firm, moist dough. Knead thoroughly. Break the dough into bread roll-size buns and place, well spaced, on an oiled baking sheet. Cover with a clean cloth and set aside to rise for another 4 hours. ❧ Bake the buns in a preheated oven at 350°F/180°C/gas 4 for about 15 minutes, or until they are well-cooked inside and golden brown on the outside.

*Serves 6*

*Preparation: 30 minutes + 7 hours' rising*

*Cooking: about 15 minutes*

*Recipe grading: fairly easy*

- 2 tablespoons/1 oz/30 g fresh compressed/baker's yeast or 3 packets active dried yeast
- scant 1 cup/7 fl oz/200 ml lukewarm water
- 2½ cups/10 oz/300 g all-purpose/plain flour
- 2 tablespoons extra-virgin olive oil
- ¼ cup/2 oz/60 g superfine/caster sugar
- ⅓ cup/3½ oz/100 g golden raisins, soaked in warm water for 15 minutes, well-drained
- 3 tablespoons pine nuts
- 1½ tablespoons chopped candied orange and lemon rinds
- salt to taste

*Suggested wine: a sweet or medium dessert wine (Marino Amabile or Dolce)*

*Maritozzi were traditionally offered to family and guests during Lent with a glass of sweet or dry white wine.*

# Fragole al Vino Bianco

## *Strawberries in White Wine*

*Serves 4*

*Preparation: 5 minutes + 1 hour's resting*

*Recipe grading: easy*

- 1¼ lb/625 g fresh strawberries
- 6 tablespoons superfine/caster sugar
- ½ cup/4 fl oz/125 ml dry white wine

*Suggested wine: a light, dry white (Frascati)*

Clean the strawberries and rinse under cold running water. Drain well, then pat dry with a clean dishcloth. ❧ Transfer the strawberries to a serving dish. Sprinkle with the sugar and drizzle with the wine. ❧ Place in the refrigerator to rest for at least 1 hour before serving.

*Healthy and delicious on their own, these strawberries are excellent when served with vanilla ice cream. They make a refreshing dessert at the end of dinner on warm, early summer nights when the strawberry season is at its peak. Try replacing the wine with the same amount of white wine vinegar for even more taste.*

# Crema di Ricotta
## *Ricotta Cream*

Put the ricotta in a mixing bowl and stir in the confectioners' sugar and cinnamon. Mix well to obtain a smooth, light cream. ➣ Place in the refrigerator to rest for at least 1 hour before serving.

*Serves 4*

*Preparation: 5 minutes + 1 hour's resting*

*Recipe grading: easy*

- 1¼ lb/625 g fresh ricotta cheese
- 6 tablespoons confectioners'/icing sugar
- 1 teaspoon freshly ground cinnamon

*Suggested wine: a dry, sparkling white (Colli Albani Spumante Secco)*

*This recipe calls for the very freshest of ricotta cheese. Don't even attempt to make it with the ricotta cheeses prepacked in plastic containers. You can replace the cinnamon with ½ teaspoon of vanilla extract, or 2 tablespoons of unsweetened cocoa powder.*

# Pizza Dolce Civitavecchiese

## *Sweet Pizza from Civitavecchia*

*Serves 8–10*

*Preparation: 30 minutes + overnight rising + 3 hours' rising*

*Cooking: 40 minutes*

*Recipe grading: complicated*

- 3 tablespoons/1½ oz/45 g fresh compressed/baker's yeast or 4½ packets active dried yeast
- about 5 tablespoons water
- 3½ cups/15 oz/450 g all-purpose/plain flour
- 7 eggs
- ⅔ cup/5 oz/150 g superfine/caster sugar
- ¼ cup/2 oz/60 g fresh ricotta cheese
- scant ½ cup/3½ fl oz/100 ml rum
- scant ½ cup/3½ fl oz/100 ml milk
- 1 teaspoon ground cinnamon
- ½ teaspoon crushed aniseed seeds
- grated rind of 1 lemon
- scant ½ cup/3½ fl oz/100 g lard (or butter), softened
- 5 tablespoons confectioners'/icing sugar

*Suggested wine: a sweet dessert wine (Aleatico di Gradoli)*

Crumble the yeast into a small bowl with the water, stirring until the yeast dissolves. ❧ Leave to stand for 10 minutes in a warm (not hot) place until the surface is frothy. ❧ Put about a quarter of the flour in a mixing bowl and stir in the yeast mixture. Transfer to a lightly floured work surface and knead to obtain a smooth dough. Form the dough into a ball, then cover with a clean cloth and set aside to rise overnight. ❧ Next morning, separate the eggs and beat 6 yolks with the sugar in a large mixing bowl until smooth and creamy. ❧ Whisk the 7 egg whites until they form stiff peaks. ❧ Stir the ricotta, rum, milk, egg whites, cinnamon, aniseed, and lemon rind into the egg yolk and sugar mixture. ❧ Mix well, then add the risen dough, the remaining flour, and the lard (or butter). Turn the mixture out onto a floured work surface and knead for about 10 minutes. Form the dough into a ball, then cover with a clean cloth and set aside in a warm place to rise for 2 hours. ❧ Knead again for a few minutes, and form into a ball. Set aside as before to rise for 1 hour. ❧ Place the dough in a large buttered springform pan (tin). Beat the remaining egg yolk and pour it over the top. Sprinkle with the confectioners' sugar. ❧ Bake in a preheated oven at 325°F/160°C/gas 3 for 40 minutes or until well browned on top. ❧ Remove from the springform pan and leave to cool.

*Making this special cake is a marathon job, but well worth the effort!*

# Dolci

# Sformato al Cioccolato
## Chocolate Mold

Serves 6
Preparation: 30 minutes
Cooking: 25 minutes
Recipe grading: fairly easy

- ½ cup/2 oz/60 g all-purpose/plain flour
- 1 cup/8 fl oz/250 ml milk
- ½ cup/4 oz/125 g superfine/caster sugar
- ½ stick/2 oz/60 g butter
- 4 eggs, separated
- 5 tablespoons unsweetened cocoa powder

Suggested wine: a dry sparkling white (Frascati Spumante)

Mix the flour in a little of the milk until smooth. ❧ Bring the remaining milk to a boil in a heavy-bottomed saucepan with the sugar and butter. Stir in the flour mixture and mix well. Remove from the heat and set aside to cool. ❧ Beat the egg yolks until creamy. ❧ Whisk the egg whites until they form stiff peaks. ❧ Add the cocoa powder to the cooled milk mixture and mix well. ❧ Stir in the egg yolks, then fold the egg whites in carefully. ❧ Butter and flour a ring mold and pour the mixture into it. ❧ Bake in a preheated oven at 375°F/190°C/gas 5 for 25 minutes. ❧ Remove from the oven and set aside to cool. Turn out of the ring mold and serve.

This delicious mold will be a hit with all chocolate lovers. If liked, it can be kept in the refrigerator for a few hours before serving.

108

# La Dolce Vita

Italian film director Federico Fellini immortalized the life and times of the international set of "beautiful" people in Rome in the late 1950s in his satirical film *La Dolce Vita* (1960). During the 1950s and 60s Rome became the Hollywood of Europe, particularly as American film makers took advantage of lower costs and taxes by making their films in Italy. This is the era of the "Spaghetti Western". The actors, actresses, directors, and film crews that flocked to the city added another dimension to the capital's social and nightlife which was already populated by a heterogenous group of Italian and European artists and intellectuals. Much of the action was centered on Via Veneto, which at that time was a smart area with upmarket hotels, restaurants, and cafés. (It has since lost its position as the meeting place of the idle rich and the famous). The Piazza di Spagna area, also mentioned in the film, is still a lively part of town with some excellent shopping (the via Condotti is perhaps the most famous area for fashion and design) as well as cafés and restaurants. Both the Via Veneto and Piazza di Spagna quarters are still popular today, although some other new areas have opened up in the meantime. The narrow streets and charming piazzas of Trastevere, and the areas around Piazza Navona, and the Pantheon are always good bets for food and nightlife.

During the 18th century, when Rome was one of the focal points of the Grand Tour taken by well-to-do Europeans, the area around Piazza di Spagna (the Spanish Steps) was the "in" place to be seen. Then, as now, both tourists and locals spent a lot of time in the cafés, chatting and people-watching.

The film poster from La Dolce Vita, *which starred blonde bombshell Anita Ekberg and handsome Marcello Mastroiani.*

In a city of fountains the Trevi Fountain is perhaps the most famous of them all. Traditionally the spot to toss a coin over one's back while making the wish to return again to Rome, it was made even more famous by Fellini's film. It was here that Anita Ekberg took her cooling midnight dip with Mastroianni in attendance.

The Café de Paris opened its doors in Via Veneto in 1956. It was one of the best cafés during the area's heyday. The whole area is (at least in Roman terms) quite recent; most of it was laid out after Rome became capital of Italy in 1870. A restaurant called George's at number 7 in Via Marche (parallel to Via Veneto) is another good place to capture some of the flavor of the dolce vita times.

Big names in the Italian fashion world line the streets of central Rome.

# Ciambelline Dolci

*Sweet Rings*

*Serves 6*

*Preparation: 15 minutes + 1 hour's resting*

*Cooking: 25 minutes*

*Recipe grading: easy*

- 3 cups/10 oz/300 g all-purpose/plain flour
- scant 1 cup/7 oz/200 g superfine/caster sugar
- 2–3 drops vanilla extract/essence
- 1 teaspoon ground cinnamon
- finely grated rind of 1 lemon
- 1 teaspoon baking powder
- 3 tablespoons extra-virgin olive oil
- 2 eggs
- butter and flour for the baking sheet(s)

*Suggested wine: a sweet white (Orvieto Dolce)*

Place the flour, sugar, vanilla, cinnamon, lemon rind, and baking powder in a mixing bowl. Stir in the oil and eggs and mix for about 5–8 minutes with a wooden spoon. Cover with a clean cloth and leave to rest for 1 hour. ❧ Lightly flour a clean work surface and shape pieces of dough into long, thin sausages. Cut into lengths of about 4 in/10 cm and press the ends of each length together to form a ring. ❧ Transfer the rings to a buttered and floured baking sheet. ❧ Bake in a preheated oven at 400°F/200°C/gas 6 for 25 minutes. ❧ Cool on a wire rack.

*These simple and delicious little cookies are excellent to serve with coffee or tea.*

# Bigné di San Giuseppe
## *Lemon and Egg Fritters*

Place the water, salt, butter, sugar, and lemon rind in a heavy-bottomed saucepan and bring to a boil. ❧ When the water is boiling, add the flour and stir with a wooden spoon. Continue cooking, stirring continuously, until the dough is thick and comes away from the sides of the saucepan. Remove from the heat and set aside to cool. ❧ When cool, stir in the eggs one at a time. The dough should be soft, but not runny. ❧ Set aside to rest for at least 1 hour. ❧ Heat the oil in a deep-sided skillet (frying pan) until very hot, but not smoking. ❧ Use a teaspoon to scoop up the dough and drop it into the hot oil. Fry the fritters, a few at a time, until they are plump and golden brown. ❧ Remove the fritters from the oil with a slotted spoon and drain on paper towels. Keep warm. Repeat until all the dough has been used up. ❧ Sprinkle with confectioners' sugar and serve hot.

*Serves 4–6*

*Preparation: 25 minutes + 1 hour's resting*

*Cooking: 25 minutes*

*Recipe grading: fairly easy*

- 1 cup/8 fl oz/250 ml water
- dash of salt
- 1 stick/4 oz/125 g butter
- $1/4$ cup/2 oz/60 g superfine/caster sugar
- finely grated rind of 1 lemon
- 2 cups/8 oz/250 g all-purpose/plain flour
- 8 eggs
- 1–2 cups/8–16 fl oz/250–500 ml olive oil for frying
- confectioners'/icing sugar for sprinkling

*Suggested wine: a sweet white (Orvieto Dolce)*

*These fritters are traditionally served on 19 March – St. Joseph's Day – but they are delicious all year round.*

# Pesche al Forno

## *Stuffed Baked Peaches*

Wash the peaches under cold running water. Dry well and cut them in half. ❧ Remove the stone and use a teaspoon to hollow out a hole about the size of a golf ball from the centers. ❧ Place the peach flesh in a bowl and add three-quarters of the amaretti cookies and all but 4 tablespoons of the sugar. Mix well and use the mixture to fill the peaches. ❧ Spread the butter over the bottom of an ovenproof dish large enough to hold all the peach halves quite snugly. Arrange the peaches in it. ❧ Drizzle with the rum and sprinkle with the remaining amaretti cookies and sugar. ❧ Bake in a preheated oven at 350°F/180°C/gas 4 for 30 minutes. ❧ Serve hot or warm.

*Serves 4–6*
*Preparation: 25 minutes*
*Cooking: 30 minutes*
*Recipe grading: fairly easy*

- 4–6 large ripe peaches
- 3½ oz/100 g amaretti cookies, crushed
- ⅔ cup/5 oz/150 g sugar superfine/ caster sugar
- ¼ stick/1 oz/30 g butter
- 4 tablespoons dark rum

*Suggested wine: a sweet dessert white*
*(Colli Albani Dolce Superiore)*

*The sweet almondy taste of the amaretti cookies blends perfectly with the peaches and rum. Use more or less sugar depending on how sweet you like it. These are excellent with whipped cream or ice cream.*

# Fave Dolci
## *Almond Cookies*

*Serves 8–10*
*Preparation: 20 minutes*
*Cooking: 20 minutes*
*Recipe grading: easy*

- 1 cup/4 oz/125 g whole blanched almonds
- 2/3 cup/5 oz/150 g superfine/caster sugar
- scant 1 cup/3 1/2 oz/100 g all-purpose/plain flour
- 1/2 stick/2 oz/60 g butter
- 1 teaspoon ground cinnamon
- 1 egg
- grated rind of 1/2 lemon

*Suggested wine: a sweet dessert wine (Aleatico di Gradoli)*

Spread the almonds in a large baking pan and toast in a preheated oven at 350°F/180°C/gas 4 for around 8 minutes, or until the almonds are just beginning to color. Remove from the oven and set aside to cool. Combine the cooled almonds with half the sugar in a food processor fitted with a steel blade. Process until the almonds are ground to a powder. Place the almonds and sugar in a mixing bowl and stir in three-quarters of the flour, the butter, the cinnamon, egg, and lemon rind. Mix well to obtain a smooth, firm dough. Use the remaining flour to lightly flour a clean work surface and shape the dough into a long sausage. Slice crosswise to obtain small, oval cookies. Sprinkle with the remaining sugar. Transfer the cookies to a greased and floured baking sheet and bake in a preheated oven at 300°F/150°C/gas 2 for 20 minutes, or until the cookies are light golden brown. Remove from the sheet and set aside to cool on a wire rack. After a few hours they will be crisp. Store in an airtight cookie jar.

*These cookies are called* fave *(fava beans or broad beans) because of their shape. They are also called All Soul's Cookies because they are traditionally served in early November to celebrate the Roman Catholic feast day.*

# Index

# Index

# Acknowledgments

The Publishers would like to thank Mastrociliegia, Fiesole (Florence) and Bottega della Pasta (Florence) who kindly lent props for photography.

All photos by MARCO LANZA except:

FARABOLAFOTO, MILAN: 1, 6, 37TR; GIUSEPPE CARFAGNA, ROME: 2, 3, 9, 11, 12, 13, 22, 23, 36B, 37TL, 37B, 43, 60, 66B, 75B, 79, 82, 83, 88, 89, 110TR, 110B; MARCO NARDI: COVER, 7B, 38, 44, 67, 111 TL, 108.

ILLUSTRATIONS: LORENZO CECCHI 75 TL; PAOLA HOLGUÍN 67TL; SABRINA MARCONI 67CR, 67B; IVAN STALIO 5, 36T, 66T, 67CL, 75TR, 110.